T0306543

OBADIAH

OBADIAH
The Kingship Belongs to YHWH

SECOND EDITION

ZONDERVAN
Exegetical
Commentary
ON THE
Old Testament
A DISCOURSE ANALYSIS OF THE HEBREW BIBLE

DANIEL I. BLOCK

DANIEL I. BLOCK
General Editor

The Hebrew text on the cover is from Deuteronomy 31:11–13, which highlights the importance of "hearing" the voice of Scripture:

When all Israel comes to appear before the YHWH your God at the place he will choose, you shall read this Torah before them in their hearing. Assemble the people—men, women and children, and the foreigners residing in your towns—so they can *listen* and learn to fear the YHWH your God and follow carefully all the words of this Torah. Their children, who do not know this Torah, must *hear* it and learn to fear the YHWH your God as long as you live in the land you are crossing the Jordan to possess. (NIV, modified)

ZONDERVAN

Obadiah
Copyright © 2013, 2017 by Daniel I. Block

Requests for information should be addressed to:

Zondervan, 3900 Sparks Dr. SE, Grand Rapids, Michigan 49546

ISBN: 978-0-310-57153-7

Cover design: Tammy Johnson
Cover photography: The Bridgeman Art Library; Masterfile; iStockphoto
Interior illustration/production: Beth Shagene
Interior design: Beth Shagene

Printed in the United States of America

17 18 19 20 21 22 23 24 /DHV/ 25 24 23 22 21 20 19 18 17 16 15 14 13 12 11 10 9 8 7 6 5 4 3 2 1

This book is dedicated to Bud and Betty Knoedler,
my friends in Christ and in his service

Contents

Series Introduction

Prospectus

Modern audiences are often taken in by the oratorical skill and creativity of preachers and teachers. However, they tend to forget that the authority of proclamation is directly related to the correspondence of the key points of the sermon to the message the biblical authors were trying to communicate. Since we confess that all Scripture [including the entirety of the OT] is God-breathed and useful for teaching, rebuking, correcting and training in righteous ness, so that [all God's people] may be thoroughly equipped for every good work" (2 Tim 3:16 – 17 NIV), it seems essential that those who proclaim its message should pay close attention to the rhetorical agendas of biblical authors. Too often modern readers, including preachers, are either baffled by OT texts, or they simply get out of them that for which they are looking. Many commentaries available to pastors and teachers try to resolve the dilemma either through word-by-word and verse-by-verse analysis or synthetic theological reflections on the text without careful attention to the flow and argument of that text.

The commentators in this series recognize that too little attention has been paid to biblical authors as rhetoricians, to their larger rhetorical and theological agendas, and especially to the means by which they tried to achieve their goals. Like effective communicators in every age, biblical authors were driven by a passion to communicate a message. So we must inquire not only what that message was, but also what strategies they used to impress their message on their hearers' ears. This reference to "hearers" rather than to readers is intentional, since the biblical texts were written to be heard. Not only were the Hebrew and Christian Scriptures composed to be heard in the public gathering of God's people, but also before the invention of moveable type few would have had access to their own copies of the Scriptures. While the contributors to this series acknowledge with Paul that every Scripture — that is, every passage in the Hebrew Bible — is God-breathed, we also recognize that the inspired authors possessed a vast repertoire of rhetorical and literary strategies. These included not only the special use of words and figures of speech, but also the deliberate selection, arrangement, and shaping of ideas.

The primary goal of this commentary series is to help serious students of Scripture, as well as those charged with preaching and teaching the Word of God, to hear the messages of Scripture as biblical authors intended them to be heard. While we recognize the timelessness of the biblical message, the validity of our interpretation and the authority with which we teach the Scriptures are related directly to the extent to which we have grasped the message intended by the author in the first place. Accordingly, when dealing with specific texts, the authors of the commentaries in this series are concerned with three principal questions: (1) What are the principal theological points the biblical writers are making? (2) How do biblical writers make those points? (3) What significance does the message of the present text have for understanding the message of the biblical book within which it is embedded and the message of the Scriptures as a whole. The achievement of these goals requires careful attention to the way ideas are expressed in the OT, including the selection and arrangement of materials and the syntactical shaping of the text.

To most readers syntax operates primarily at the sentence level. But recent developments in biblical study, particularly advances in rhetorical and discourse analysis, have alerted us to the fact that syntax operates also at the levels of the paragraph, the literary unit being analyzed, and the composition as a whole. Discourse analysis, also called macro syntax, studies the text beyond the level of the sentence (sentence syntax), where the paragraph serves as the basic unit of thought. Those contributing to this series recognize that this type of study may be pursued in a variety of ways. Some will prefer a more bottom-up approach, where clause connectors and transitional features play a dominant role in analysis. Others will pursue a more top-down approach, where genre or literary form begins the discussion. However, we all understand that both approaches are required to understand fully the method and the message of the text. For this reason, the ultimate value of discourse analysis is that it allows the text to set the agenda in biblical interpretation.

One of the distinctive goals for this series is to engage the biblical text using some form of discourse analysis to understand not only what the text says, but also how it says it. While attention to words or phrases is still essential, contributors to this commentary series will concentrate on the flow of thought in the biblical writings, both at the macroscopic level of entire compositions and at the microscopic level of individual text units. In so doing we hope to help other readers of Scripture grasp both the message and the rhetorical force of Old Testament texts. When we hear the message of Scripture, we gain access to the mind of God.

Format of the Commentary

The format of this series is designed to achieve the goals summarized above. Accordingly, each volume in the series will begin with an introduction to the book being explored. In addition to answering the usual questions of date, authorship, and provenance of the composition, commentators will highlight what they consider to be the main theological themes of the book, and then discuss broadly how the style and structure of the book develop those themes. This discussion will include a coherent outline of the contents of the book, demonstrating the contribution each part makes to the development of the principal themes.

The commentaries on individual text units that follow will repeat this process in greater detail. Although complex literary units will be broken down further, the commentators will address the following issues.

1. **The Main Idea of the Passage**: A one- or two-sentence summary of the key ideas the biblical author seeks to communicate.

2. **Literary Context**: A brief discussion of the relationship of the specific text to the book as a whole and to its place within the broader arguments.

3. **Translation and Exegetical Outline**: Commentators will provide their own translations of each text, formatted to highlight the discourse structure of the text and accompanied by a coherent outline that reflects the flow and argument of the text.

4. **Structure and Literary Form**: An introductory survey of the literary structure and rhetorical style adopted by the biblical author, highlighting how these features contribute to the communication of the main idea of the passage.

5. **Explanation of the Text**: A detailed commentary on the passage, paying particular attention to how the biblical authors select and arrange their materials and how they work with words, phrases, and syntax to communicate their messages. This will take up the bulk of most commentaries.

6. **Canonical and Practical Significance**: The commentary on each unit will conclude by building bridges between the world of the biblical author and other biblical authors and with reflections on the contribution made by this unit to the development of broader issues in biblical theology — particularly on how later OT and NT authors have adapted and reused the motifs in question. The discussion will also include brief reflections on the significance of the message of the passage for readers today.

The way this series treats biblical books will be uneven. Commentators on smaller books will have sufficient scope to answer fully each of the issues listed above on each unit of text. However, limitations of space preclude full treatment of every text for the larger books. Instead, commentators will guide readers through ## 1 – 4 and 6 for every literary unit, but "Full Explanation of the Text" (#5) will be selective, generally limited to twelve to fifteen literary units deemed most critical for hearing the message of the book.

In addition to these general introductory comments, we should alert readers of this series to several conventions that we follow. First, unless otherwise indicated, the English translations of biblical texts are the commentators' own.

Second, the divine name in the OT is presented as YHWH. The form of the name — represented by the Tetragrammaton, יהוה — is a particular problem for scholars. The practice of rendering the divine name in Greek as κύριος (= Heb. אֲדֹנָי, "Adonay") is carried over into English translations as "LORD" or "LORD," which reflects the Hebrew יהוה, and distinguishes it from "Lord," which reflects Hebrew אֲדֹנָי. But this creates interpretive problems, for the connotations and implications of referring to someone by name or by title are quite different. When rendered as a name, English translations have traditionally vocalized יהוה as "Jehovah," which combines the consonants of יהוה with the vowels of אֲדֹנָי. However, today non-Jewish scholars often render the name as "Yahweh," recognizing that "Jehovah" is an artificial construct.

Third, frequently the verse numbers in the Hebrew Bible differ from those in our English translations. Since the commentaries in this series are based on the Hebrew text, the Hebrew numbers will be the default numbers. Where the English numbers differ, they will be provided in square brackets (e.g., Joel 4:12[3:12]).

Fourth, when discussing specific biblical words or phrases, these will be represented in Hebrew font and in translation, except where the transliterated form is used in place of an English term, either because no single English expression captures the Hebrew word's wide range meaning (e.g., *ḥesed* for חֶסֶד, rather than "lovingkindness"), or when it functions as a title or technical expression not readily captured in English (e.g., *gōʾēl* for גֹּאֵל, rather than "kinsman redeemer").

Author's Preface and Acknowledgments

With this volume we are launching a new commentary series whose goal is to help readers of the Scriptures hear the messages that the human and divine authors intended to communicate. We will do so not only by declaring to readers of these commentaries our conclusions on what those messages are, but also by paying careful attention to the literary, discourse, and rhetorical strategies employed by the inspired authors to get their message across.

The book of Obadiah offers a convenient place to start because it is a short, manageable text and because it is driven by a profound theology of hope. Having spent many years producing commentaries on lengthy books like Ezekiel, Judges, and Deuteronomy, it has been a delight to wrestle with this miniature book and to discover the sophistication of Obadiah's literary style and the profundity of his theology. I pray that my work will aid us all in hearing its message and glorifying God for his steadfast love to his people.

My work on Obadiah started in 2009, when I had the privilege of team-teaching a Hebrew exegesis course on Jonah and Obadiah with two of my doctoral students, Jason Gile and Charlie Trimm. I am grateful for the insights I received from my students. I am also deeply appreciative for work of my assistants, Carmen Imes and Austin Surls, in editing and proofreading drafts of this manuscript and for their aid in preparing the indexes. I must also express my gratitude for the encouragement and responses to my work by the members of the ZECOT Editorial Committee. The entire editorial team is grateful for the support of this series that we have received from Stan Gundry, Katya Covrett, and Verlyn Verbrugge. Verlyn's meticulous editorial work has spared us unnecessary embarrassment and greatly enhanced the quality of the final product.

I would be remiss if I did not express gratitude to my administration and my faculty colleagues at Wheaton College for creating an atmosphere that encourages scholarship in the service of the church and for encouraging us as we seek to play a small role in this venture. Special thanks are due to Bud and Betty Knoedler, my dear friends who have generously endowed the chair I occupy at Wheaton College, providing me with resources and time to pursue my research. This book is dedicated to them with deep affection and respect.

However, no human being deserves more credit for whatever I have been able to contribute to the work of Christ and his kingdom than my wife, Ellen, who has stood by me for forty-six years and brought me so much joy. Nevertheless, the ultimate credit for any positive contribution we might have made to the church and to the scholarly enterprise must go to YHWH, the God of Israel, incarnate in Jesus Christ. The dominion belongs to him (Obad 21), so to him be all the praise, the renown, and the glory (Deut 26:19).

DANIEL BLOCK
July, 2012

Abbreviations

Abbreviations for books of the Bible, pseudepigrapha, rabbinic works, papyri, classical works, and the like are readily available in sources such as the *SBL Handbook of Style* and are not included here.

AASOR	Annual of the American Schools of Oriental Research
AB	Anchor Bible
ABD	*Anchor Bible Dictionary*, ed. David Noel Freedman.
ANE	Ancient Near East, Ancient Near Eastern
ANEP	*The Ancient Near East in Pictures Relating to the Old Testament*, ed. J. B. Pritchard.
ANET	*Ancient Near Eastern Texts Relating to the Old Testament*, ed. J. B. Pritchard, 3rd ed.
ARAB	*Ancient Records of Assyria and Babylonia*, ed. Daniel D. Luckenbill.
ATD	Das Alte Testament Deutsch
BASOR	*Bulletin of the American Schools of Oriental Research*
BHS	Biblia Hebraica Stuttgartensia
BHQ	Biblia Hebraica quinta
Bib	*Biblica*
BIS	Biblical Interpretation Series
BZAW	Beihefte zur Zeitschrift für die alttestamentliche Wissenschaft
CAD	*The Assyrian Dictionary of the Oriental Institute of the University of Chicago*
COS	*The Context of Scripture*, ed. W. W. Hallo.
DNWSI	*Dictionary of North-West Semitic Inscriptions*, ed. J. Hoftijzer and K. Jongeling.
ETS	Evangelical Theological Society
GKC	*Gesenius' Hebrew Grammar*, ed. E. Kautzch; trans. A. E. Cowley, 2nd ed.
HALOT	*The Hebrew and Aramaic Lexicon of the Old Testament*, ed. L. Koehler, W. Baumgartner, and J. J. Stamm.
HSM	Harvard Semitic Monographs
HTR	*Harvard Theological Review*

IOS	*Israel Oriental Studies*
ISBE	*International Standard Bible Encyclopedia*, ed. G. W. Bromiley, 2nd ed.
JBL	*Journal of Biblical Literature*
JETS	*Journal of the Evangelical Theological Society*
JM	*A Grammar of Biblical Hebrew*, by Paul Joüon; trans. and rev. by T. Muraoka.
JNES	*Journal of Near Eastern Studies*
JSOT	*Journal for the Study of the Old Testament*
JSOTSup	Journal for the Study of the Old Testament Supplement series
JTT	*Journal of Translation and Textlinguistics*
KAI	*Kanaanäische und aramäische Inschriften*, ed. H. Donner and W. Röllig, 2nd ed.
NASB	New American Standard Bible
NICOT	New International Commentary on the Old Testament
NIV	New International Version
NIVAC	NIV Application Commentaries
NRSV	New Revised Standard Version
OBO	Orbis biblicus et orientalis
OTL	Old Testament Library
PL	Patrologia latina, ed. J.-P. Migne.
SBLDS	Society of Biblical Literature Dissertation Series
SBLSymS	Society of Biblical Literature Symposium Series
SBLWAW	Society of Biblical Literature Writings from the Ancient World
SR	*Studies in Religion*
TA	*Tel Aviv*
THAT	*Theologisches Handwörterbuch zum Alten Testament*, ed. E. Jenni and C. Westermann.
TLOT	*Theological Lexicon of the Old Testament*, ed. E. Jenni and C. Westermann, trans. M. E. Biddle.
TNK	Tanak, the Jewish Bible
UF	*Ugarit-Forschungen*
VT	*Vetus Testamentum*
VTSup	Supplements to Vetus Testamentum
ZAW	*Zeitschrift für die alttestamentliche Wissenschaft*

Select Bibliography

Ackroyd, Peter R. "Obadiah, Book of." *ABD*, 5:2 – 4.

Allen, Leslie C. *The Books of Joel, Obadiah, Jonah, and Micah*. NICOT. Grand Rapids: Eerdmans, 1976.

Armerding, Carl E. "Obadiah." Pages 421 – 50 in *The Expositor's Bible Commentary*. Vol. 8. Edited by T. Longman III and David Garland. Grand Rapids: Zondervan, 2008.

Baker, David W. "Obadiah." In *Obadiah, Jonah, Micah*. TOTC. Downers Grove, IL: InterVarsity Press, 1988.

Bartlett, John R. "The Brotherhood of Edom." *JSOT* 4 (1977): 2 – 27.

———. *Edom and the Edomites*. JSOTSup 77. Sheffield: JSOT, 1989.

Barton, John. *Joel and Obadiah: A Commentary*. OTL. Louisville: Westminster John Knox, 2001.

Ben Zvi, Ehud. *A Historical-Critical Study of the Book of Obadiah*. BZAW 242. Berlin/New York: de Gruyter, 1996.

Block, Daniel I. *The Book of Ezekiel Chapters 1 – 24*. NICOT. Grand Rapids: Eerdmans, 1997.

———. *The Book of Ezekiel Chapters 25 – 48*. NICOT. Grand Rapids: Eerdmans, 1998.

———. *Deuteronomy*. NIVAC. Grand Rapids: Zondervan, 2012.

Carroll, Robert P. "Obadiah." Pages 496 – 97 in *A Dictionary of Biblical Interpretation*. Edited by R. J. Coggins and J. L. Houlden. London: SCM, 1990.

Coggins, R. J. "The Minor Prophets — One Book or Twelve?" Pages 57 – 68 in *Crossing the Boundaries: Essays in Biblical Interpretation in Honour of Michael D. Goulder*. Edited by S. E. Porter, P. Joyce, and C. E. Orton. BIS 8. Leiden: Brill, 1994.

Deissler, A. *Zwölf Propheten II: Obadja, Jona, Micha, Nahum, Habakkuk*. Würzburg: Echter, 1984.

Dick, Michael B. "A Syntactic Study of the Book of Obadiah." *Semitics* 9 (1984): 1 – 29.

Follingstad, C. M. *Deictic Viewpoint in Biblical Hebrew Text: A Syntagmatic and Paradigmatic Analysis of the Particle* כִּי. Dallas: SIL, 2001.

Glazier-McDonald, B. "Edom in the Prophetical Corpus." Pages 23 – 32 in *You Shall Not Abhor an Edomite for He Is Your Brother: Edom and Seir in History and Tradition*. Edited by D. V. Edelman. Archaeology and Biblical Studies 3. Atlanta: Scholars, 1995.

House, Paul R. *The Unity of the Twelve*. JSOTSup 97. Sheffield: Almond, 1990.

Jones, Barry Alan. *The Formation of the Book of the Twelve: A Study in Text and Canon*. SBLDS 149. Atlanta: Scholars, 1995.

Kennedy, James M. "Obadiah." *ABD*, 5:1 – 2.

Limburg, James. Pages 127 – 36 in *Hosea-Micah*. Interpretation. Louisville: Westminster John Knox, 1988.

Niehaus, Jeffrey. "Obadiah." Pages 495–541 in *The Minor Prophets: An Exegetical and Expository Commentary*. Vol. 2. Edited by T. E. McComiskey. Grand Rapids: Baker, 1993.

Nogalski, James. *Literary Precursors to the Book of the Twelve*. BZAW 217. Berlin: de Gruyter, 1993.

———. *Redactional Processes in the Book of the Twelve*. BZAW 218. Berlin: de Gruyter, 1993.

Page, Frank S. "*Obadiah*." Pages 171–201 in *Amos, Obadiah, Jonah*. Edited by B. K. Smith and F. S. Page. New American Commentary 19a. Nashville: Broadman and Holman, 1995.

Pagan, Samuel. "The Book of Obadiah: Introduction, Commentary, and Reflections." Pages 433–59 in *The New Interpreter's Bible*. Vol. 7. Nashville: Abingdon, 1996.

Raabe, Paul. *Obadiah: A New Translation with Introduction and Commentary*. AB 24D. New York: Doubleday, 1996.

Renkema, Johan. *Obadiah*. Historical Commentary on the Old Testament. Leuven: Peeters, 2003.

Robinson, R. B. "Levels of Nationalization in Obadiah." *JSOT* 40 (1988): 83–97.

Rudolph, Wilhelm. "Obadja." *ZAW* 8 (= 49) (1931): 222–32.

———. *Joel-Amos-Obadja-Jonah*. KAT 13/2. Gütersloh: Mohn, 1971.

Stuart, Douglas. *Hosea-Jonah*. WBC 31. Waco, TX: Word, 1987.

Thompson, John A. "The Book of Obadiah." Pages 855–67 in *The Interpreter's Bible*. Vol. 6. New York: Abingdon, 1956.

Watts, John D. W. *Obadiah: A Critical Exegetical Commentary*. Grand Rapids: Eerdmans, 1969.

Wehrle, J. *Prophetie und Textanalyze: Die Komposition Obadja 1–21 interpretiert auf der Basis textlinguistischer und semiotischer Konzeptionen*. Abhandlungen zur Theologie des Alten und Neuen Testaments 28. St. Ottilien: EOS, 1987.

Weiser, Anton. *Das Buch der zwölf kleinen Propheten I: Die Propheten Hosea Hosea, Joel, Obadja, Jona, Micha*. 5th ed. ATD 24. Göttingen: Vandenhoeck & Ruprecht, 1967.

Wendland, Ernst. "Obadiah's 'Day': On the Rhetorical Influence of Textual Form and Intertextual Influence." *JTT* 8 (1996): 45–47.

———. *Prophetic Rhetoric: Case Studies in Text Analysis and Translation*. N.p.: Xulon, 2009.

Wolff, Hans Walther. "Obadja — Ein Kultprophet als Interpret." *Evangelische Theologie* 37 (1977): 273–84.

———. *Obadiah and Jonah: A Commentary*. Trans. M. Kohl. Minneapolis: Augsburg, 1986.

Translation of Obadiah 1 – 21

¹The vision of Obadiah.

Thus says Adonay YHWH concerning Edom:

A report we have heard from YHWH, and an envoy has been sent among the nations: "Rise up!"

"Yes, let us rise against her for battle!"

²See, small I have made you among the nations; you are utterly despised. ³The smugness of your heart has deceived you, the one who lives in the clefts of the rock, in your lofty dwelling, who says in his heart, "Who will bring me down to earth?"

⁴If you elevate [it] like a vulture, and if among the stars one sets your nest, from there I will bring you down — the declaration of YHWH.

⁵If thieves came to you, if burglars at night — ah, how you have been destroyed! — would they not steal enough for themselves? If grape gatherers came to you, would they not leave gleanings? ⁶Ah, how Esau has been hunted down, his storerooms ransacked!

⁷To the border all your allies have sent you; they have deceived you; your allies have prevailed against you; [those who eat] your bread have set a trap beneath you — he has no clue!

⁸Will not on that day — the declaration of YHWH — I destroy the wise from Edom, and understanding from Mount Esau? ⁹Then your heroes will panic, O Teman, so every man will be cut off from Mount Esau. ¹⁰Because of murder, violence against your brother Jacob, shame shall cover you, and you shall be cut off forever.

¹¹On the day that you stood aloof, on the day that strangers carried off his nobility, and foreigners entered his gates, and for Jerusalem they cast lots, you too were like one of them.

¹²But you should not gloat over the day of your brother on the day of his misfortune.

And you should not rejoice over the people of Judah on the day of their ruin.

And you should not boast on the day of distress.

¹³You should not enter the gate of my people on the day of their doom.

You should not gloat — yes you — over his disaster on the day of his doom.

And you should not reach for his wealth on the day of his doom.

[14]And you should not stand at the crossroads to cut off his fugitives.

And you should not hand over his survivors on the day of distress.

[15]Surely the day of YHWH against all the nations is near. As you have done, it shall be done to you. Your action shall return on your own head. [16]Indeed as you will have drunk on my holy mountain, so all the nations shall drink to the full. They shall drink and they shall puke, and they shall be as if they had never existed.

[17]But on Mount Zion there shall be an escape, and there shall be holiness. And the house of Jacob shall possess their own possessions. [18]The house of Jacob shall be fire, and the house of Joseph [shall be] a flame, and the house of Esau [shall be] straw. They shall burn them and consume them, and there shall be no survivor for the house of Esau, for YHWH has spoken.

[19]And the Negev will possess Mount Esau, and the Shephelah [will dispossess] the Philistines. And [.......] will possess the mountain of Ephraim and the field of Samaria, and Benjamin [will possess] Gilead. [20]And as for the exiles of Halah belonging to the people of Israel, [they will dispossess] the Canaanites as far as Zarephath. And as for the exiles of Jerusalem who are in Sepharad, they will possess the towns of the Negev.

[21]Saviors will go up to Mount Zion to rule Mount Esau, and the dominion will belong to YHWH.

Introduction to Obadiah
The Kingship Belongs to YHWH

Consisting of only 291 words, Obadiah is by far the shortest book in the OT. This tractate is slightly more than half the length of Nahum, the next shortest (558 Heb. words) and 1.3 percent of Jeremiah, the longest book (21,819 Heb. words), on which it shows remarkable dependence.[1] In the Hebrew Bible (MT) Obadiah is the fourth book in a collection known as the "Book of the Twelve"; it is sandwiched between Amos and Jonah. However, in the Greek OT (LXX), Obadiah occurs between Joel and Jonah (see Table 1.1). In recent years it has become fashionable to view the Book of the Twelve as an intentional literary composition, with a coherent plot and/or themes and literary patterns signaling that those who collected these works intended the entire work to be read as a coherent corpus.[2] Accordingly, Obadiah 1 – 5, which is heavily dependent on Jeremiah 49:9, 14 – 16, has been adapted to imitate Amos 9:1 – 4, and Obadiah 8 – 14 represents a mosaic of anti-Edom oracles, drawing on Isaiah and Ezekiel and composed for the Book of the Twelve.[3]

However, this approach has recently come under increasing criticism. Not only was the arrangement of the books that make up the Book of the Twelve quite fluid in

The Placement of Joel, Obadiah, and Jonah in the Book of the Twelve	
Hebrew Old Testament	Greek Old Testament
Hosea	Hosea
Joel	Amos
Amos	Micah
Obadiah	**Joel**
Jonah	**Obadiah**
Micah	**Jonah**
Nahum	Nahum
Habakkuk	Habakkuk
Zephaniah	Zephaniah
Haggai	Haggai
Zechariah	Zechariah
Malachi	Malachi

1. According to the figures provided in *Theological Lexicon of the Old Testament* (ed. E. Jenni and C. Westermann; trans. M. E. Biddle; Peabody, MA: Hendrickson, 2007), 3:1444 – 45.

2. Paul R. House (*The Unity of the Twelve* [JSOTSup 97; Sheffield: Almond, 1990]) argues that the Book of the Twelve exhibits a coherent comic plot with the following elements: Introduction (Hosea-Joel), Complication (Amos-Micah), Crisis (Nahum-Habakkuk), Falling Action (Zephaniah), Resolution (Haggai-Malachi; see p. 124). Focusing on catchwords and catch phrases that punctuate the books, James Nogalski argues that the Book of the Twelve is an intentional literary work produced by means of a complex redactional process that was not completed until after 332 BC. See *Literary Precursors to the Book of the Twelve* (BZAW 217; Berlin: de Gruyter, 1993); idem, *Redactional Processes in the Book of the Twelve*

(BZAW 218; Berlin: de Gruyter, 1993). See also R. J. Coggins, "The Minor Prophets — One Book or Twelve?" in *Crossing the Boundaries: Essays in Biblical Interpretation in Honour of Michael D. Goulder* (ed. S. E. Porter, P. Joyce, and C. E. Orton; BIS 8; Leiden: Brill, 1994), 57 – 68. According to Barry Alan Jones (*The Formation of the Book of the Twelve: A Study in Text and Canon* [SBLDS 149; Atlanta: Scholars, 1995]), the arrangement in the MT represents the final stage in the development of the Hebrew text of the collection, incorporating Obadiah, along with Joel and Jonah, into the sequence of eighth-century-BC prophetic books.

3. Thus James Nogalski, *Redactional Processes in the Book of the Twelve* (BZAW 218; Berlin/New York: de Gruyter, 1993), 58 – 92, 276 – 77.

antiquity,[4] but MT logically places Obadiah after Amos because this book concerns Edom, which is also the subject of the last verses of Amos (9:11 – 15).[5] Although the canonical placement of Obadiah after Amos invites us to read this book in the light of Amos, more generally the separate historical and cultural circumstances of each of the prophetic books that make up the Twelve provide a more important control for the interpretation of the books than their location in the canon. In the absence of references to these prophets elsewhere, the best clues for reconstructing the circumstances for each series of utterances are found within the books themselves and in the superscriptions that open the books.

Historical Background to Obadiah's Prophecies

Even then we must ask whether the circumstances apply to the delivery of prophetic oracles or to their transcription and incorporation into the written document before us. For example, although the superscription to the book of Isaiah invites us to read the entire book as a collection of oracles by the prophet who lived at the end of the eighth century BC, it is conceivable that the present literary work, especially chapters 40 – 66, was produced in the context of the Judeans' return from exile in the middle of the sixth century BC, when the significance of these earlier prophecies was realized.

Furthermore, we may need to distinguish between the prophet responsible for the oracles in the book and the person responsible for the book as we have it. Although it may be argued that Ezekiel himself was involved in the transcription, collection, and arrangement of the oracles in the book named after him,[6] the third person introduction to Obadiah, "the vision of Obadiah," may suggest someone other than the prophet himself produced the book as we have it. We may speculate that the book was produced at a time when Edomites were a problem for those who made up the covenant community in and around Jerusalem. Although Edom as a state seems to have come to an end in mid-sixth century BC,[7] the Edomite people did not disappear until the end of the Persian period (late fourth century BC), when they were replaced by Nabatean Arabs. The reference to the Edomites (as Esau) in Malachi, which reflects conditions in the mid-fifth century BC, suggests that at this time the descendants of Esau were still recognizable, even though the land of Edom had become "a wasteland and … [a] desert for jackals" (Mal 1:3).

Indeed, the Edomites' encroachment on Judean territory is reflected in the name

---

4. In addition to the arrangements of MT and LXX, *The Ascension of Isaiah* has Obadiah in the seventh position between Jonah and Habakkuk, and the order of the first five in *The Lives of the Prophets* is Hosea, Micah, Amos, Joel, Obadiah.

5. Leslie C. Allen (*The Books of Joel, Obadiah, Jonah, and*

Micah [NICOT; Grand Rapids: Eerdmans, 1976], 129) characterizes Obadiah as "a virtual commentary on Amos 9:12."

6. See further Daniel I. Block, *The Book of Ezekiel Chapters 1 – 24* (NICOT; Grand Rapids: Eerdmans, 1997), 17 – 23.

7. See further below.

Idumea (Mark 3:8), which referred to a region in the Negev south of Judah.[8] This suggests that the messages of the prophet would have offered hope to the Judeans long after Obadiah had delivered these oracles. Accordingly, the present written record could have been produced any time from about 550 to 350 BC. Whether or not the book contains all of Obadiah's preaching we will never know. The present text may serve as a representative sampling edited for literary purposes — though the original oral flavor is still strong.

Whatever the date of the composition of the book, the oracles contained therein come from an earlier time. However, as is common, scholars are not agreed on the date or circumstances of Obadiah's preaching. Six main theories have been proposed.[9]

(1) Early ninth century BC. In Jewish tradition the present prophet is identified with the steward in the court of Ahab with the same name (1 Kgs 18:1 – 15).[10] Second Chronicles 20 links Jehoshaphat, the Judean royal counterpart to Ahab in Samaria, with a conflict against the Transjordanian states, including Mount Seir (= Edom, 20:10). However, Ahab's steward is never mentioned in this context, nor is there any hint of a threat to Jerusalem.

(2) Mid-ninth century BC.[11] According to 2 Kgs 8:20 – 22 (cf. 2 Chr 21:8 – 20), foreigners invaded Judah and carried off the palace treasures and all the members of King Jehoram's family except Jehoahaz (2 Chr 21:17). Although the narrator uses the same word for "taking captive" (שבה) as we find in Obad 11, the text is silent not only on the involvement of Edomites (the invaders were Philistines and Arabs), but also on wholesale exile of the population.

(3) Mid-eighth century BC. Second Chronicles 28 reports that during the reign of Ahaz Syria (Aram) and the forces of Israel to the north invaded Judah, resulting in a great slaughter and the removal of 200,000 captives and a great deal of booty to Samaria (vv. 5 – 8), and that Edomites and Philistines invaded Judah from the south, seizing territory in the Negev and the Shephelah and taking many Judeans captive. However, the Edomites seemed to have remained in the south and are never associated with an attack on Jerusalem.

(4) Mid-sixth century BC. Assuming that Obadiah ministered in Judah in the wake of the sacking of Jerusalem in 586 BC and in anticipation of the fall of Edom, most scholars associate the prophecies of Obadiah with those horrific events. This is my view, which I will defend in moment.

---

8. See Barry J. Beitzel, *The Moody Atlas of the Bible* (Chicago: Moody Press, 2009), 235.

9. For fuller discussion, see Paul Raabe, *Obadiah: A New Translation with Introduction and Commentary* (AB 24D; New York: Doubleday, 1996), 49 – 56.

10. *B. Sanh.* 39b. That this man's name is spelled עֹבַדְיָהוּ rather than עֹבַדְיָה is of little consequence. The former, with the longer form of the divine name YHWH, is characteristic

of preexilic names, while the latter shorter version is common in pre- and postexilic periods. In the seventh century BC short and long forms were freely interchanged. See Ziony Zevit, "A Chapter in the History of Israelite Personal Names," *BASOR* 250 (1983): 1 – 16.

11. For a recent defense of this view see Jeffrey Niehaus, "Obadiah," in *The Minor Prophets* (3 vols.; ed. T. E. McComiskey; Grand Rapids: Baker, 1993), 496 – 502.

(5) Mid-fourth century BC. A few scholars locate the prophecies considerably later to a context when Judah was under the rule of the Persians, perhaps near the time of Malachi or Nehemiah. Some associate the attack on Edom predicted in Obad 1–10 with the Nabatean Arab invasion of Edom. Others dehistoricize the book, interpreting "Edom" as a code word for the enemies of Israel in general. Ehud Ben Zvi argues that the target audience consists of a small group of highly educated literati in the Achaemenid province of Yehud, who could appreciate "puns on words, plays on sounds, ambiguities, indeterminacies and the like," and who looked forward to an ideal future when Israel's enemies would be punished and their status among the nations would be restored. Whether Obadiah was an historical prophet or a literary creation, those who produced and (re)read the book served as brokers of divine knowledge for the illiterate.[12] While it is possible that "Edom" could serve as a symbol for all Israel's enemies, the prophecies in this book seem to derive from a real person responding to real historical events.[13]

(6) A combination of (4) and (5). Some agree that Obad 1–14, 15b should be dated in the exilic period, but treat vv. 15a and 16–21 as late addition from the Persian or even Hellenistic period. Barton compares this section with Joel 3:1–4:21[2:28–3:21], which also involves "a generalized eschatological prophecy of the 'day of YHWH.'" Here all the nations are forced to drink the cup of divine wrath imposed on Edom, and Israel and Judah are not only restored to their former territories, but their territories are also enlarged.[14] However, no details of vv. 15a and 16–21 demand such a late date.[15] Furthermore, that Obadiah should generalize Edom's judgment to that of all Israel's enemies accords with common prophetic practice, viewing specific immediate events as paradigmatic of universal truth.

As suggested above, the prophecies of Obadiah are best dated to the exilic period, specifically the period between the fall of Jerusalem in 586 BC and Edom's demise at the hands of the Babylonians in 553 BC. The terminus a quo (earliest possible date) is established by the image the prophet paints of Jerusalem and her population. Verse 11 speaks of a city that has been invaded by foreigners (נָכְרִים) and its wealth carried off; competing forces were casting lots for the booty. Verses 12–14 characterize that event as a day of misfortune (נֵכֶר, 12b), ruin, perishing (אָבַד, 12d), distress (צָרָה, 12f, 14d), doom (אֵיד, 13b, 13f), and disaster (רָעָה, 13c). Verse 16 speaks of that day as "drinking" the cup of divine fury. The image of restoration in v. 19 assumes that the territories of Ephraim, Samaria, and Gilead have been lost (to the Assyrians in 732 and 722 BC). While the "exiles of [this host] belonging to the people of Israel" in

---

12. Ehud Ben Zvi, *A Historical-Critical Study of the Book of Obadiah* (BZAW 242; Berlin/New York: de Gruyter, 1996), 260–61.

13. So also John Barton (*Joel and Obadiah: A Commentary* [OTL; Louisville: Westminster John Knox, 2001], 122), par-

ticularly with reference to Obad 1–14, 15b-d.

14. Ibid., 123.

15. Barton (ibid., 155–56) mistakenly insists that the reference to Sepharad in v. 20c demands a later date. For discussion and response, see the commentary below.

v. 20 could refer to other invasions, an allusion to the Babylonian exile seems the most natural reading. Obadiah does not refer explicitly to the destruction of the temple, but the reference to Zion as a place of refuge and a holy place alludes to the shattered hopes of the Judeans, who had viewed the temple as a symbol of security and YHWH's unqualified support in 596 BC.

The image of Edom in Obadiah reinforces the link with the collapse of the Judean state at the hands of the Babylonians. Although the conflict between the descendants of Esau and Jacob has ancient roots and is well documented elsewhere (Amos 1:11 – 12; Ezek 25:12 – 14; 35:5a), so is Edom's response to Judah in the face of her deepest crisis.[16] Ezekiel accuses Edom of handing over the people of Israel to the sword at the time of their calamity (אֵד) and their final punishment (עֲוֹן קֵץ, 35:5), of claiming the emptied lands of Judah and Israel as their own (v. 10), of expressing anger, envy, and hatred toward them (v. 11), and of taunting and celebrating over the desolation of the land (vv. 12, 15; cf. 36:2).[17] In Joel 4:19[3:19] the prophet lays specific and serious charges against Edom:

> Egypt shall become a desolation
>> and Edom a desolate wilderness,
> because of the violence done to the people of Judah,
>> in whose land they have shed innocent blood. (NRSV)

This picture accords with that of the psalmist, who recalls Edom's role with intense bitterness:

> Remember, O YHWH, against the Edomites
>> the day of Jerusalem's fall,
> how they said, "Tear it down! Tear it down!
>> Down to its foundations!"
> O daughter Babylon, you devastator!
>> Happy shall be they who pay you back
>> what you have done to us!
> Happy shall be they who take your little ones
>> and dash them against the rock! (Ps 137:7 – 9 NRSV)

The fourth lament in Lamentations also recalls Edom's involvement in Judah's demise and declares hope in her punishment:

> Rejoice and be glad, O daughter Edom,
>> you that live in the land of Uz;

16. For fuller discussion of the biblical texts, see John R. Bartlett, *Edom and the Edomites* (JSOTSup 77; Sheffield: JSOT, 1989), 151 – 57.

17. Apparently Edom was not alone in her taunts. Elsewhere we also read of the taunts of Moab and Ammon (Ezek. 25:3, 8; Zeph. 2:8), and of the Ammonites claiming Israelite territory (Jer 49:1).

but to you also the cup shall pass;
    you shall become drunk and strip yourself bare.
The punishment of your iniquity, O daughter Zion, is accomplished,
    he will keep you in exile no longer;
but your iniquity, O daughter Edom, he will punish,
    he will uncover your sins. (Lam 4:21 – 22, NRSV)

To these poetic and prophetic texts we may add the narrative of the aftermath of
the appointment of Gedaliah as governor after the fall of Jerusalem in Jer 40:11 – 12:

> Likewise, when all the Judeans who were in Moab and among the Ammonites and in
> Edom and in other lands heard that the king of Babylon had left a remnant in Judah
> and had appointed Gedaliah son of Ahikam son of Shaphan as governor over them,
> then all the Judeans returned from all the places to which they had been scattered
> and came to the land of Judah, to Gedaliah at Mizpah; and they gathered wine and
> summer fruits in great abundance. (NRSV)

Apparently, despite the nation of Edom's traditional hostility toward Judah, individual Judeans had sought and found refuge in the Transjordan, which Nebuchadnezzar's forces did not attack in 598 – 597 BC.

To these biblical sources we may now add significant supporting archaeological
data. First, Arad Ostracon 24, dated early in the sixth century BC, contains an ur-
gent request to Eliashib for troops to be sent to Arad and Ramath-negev to forestall
Edomite aggression in the Negev: "lest Edom should go there."[18] Second, dated about
the same time, an ostracon discovered in the fort of Horvat ʿUza, ca. 6 km. southeast
of Tel Arad, contains a letter from one Edomite official, Lumalak, to another, Blbl,
inscribed with a blessing in the name of Qaus, the patron deity of Edom, and a request for food supplies.[19] Third, among other inscriptions, a fragmentary ostracon
from Horvat Qitmit, an Edomite settlement 10 km. south of Tel Arad, contains the
name of the Edomite deity Qaus (קוס).[20] Fourth, the excavations at Horvat Qitmit
provide firm evidence for an Edomite shrine at this place, complete with figurines
and other cult objects.[21] This extrabiblical evidence confirms that the Edomites were
indeed poised to mock the Judeans as they fell to the Babylonians and to encroach
on their territory.

---

18. For text and commentary, see F. W. Dobbs-Allsopp et al., *Hebrew Inscriptions: Texts from the Biblical Period of the Monarchy with Concordance* (New Haven, CT: Yale Univ. Press, 2005), 47 – 53.

19. See Itzhaq Beit-Arieh, "New Data on the Relationship between Judah and Edom toward the End of the Iron Age," in *Recent Excavations in Israel: Studies in Iron Age Archaeology* (ed. S. Gitin and W. G. Dever; AASOR 49; Winona Lake, IN: Eisenbrauns, 1989), 125 – 26; Itzhaq Beit-Arieh and B. Cres-

son, "An Edomite Ostracon from Horvat ʿUza," *TA* 12 (1985): 96 – 101.

20. See Itzhaq Beit-Arieh, "Inscriptions," in *Horvat Qitmit: An Edomite Shrine in the Biblical Negev* (ed. I. Beit-Arieh; Monograph Series of the Institute of Archaeology 11; Tel Aviv: Tel Aviv University, 1995), 260 – 61.

21. The entire volume cited above, *Horvat Qitmit: An Edomite Shrine in the Biblical Negev*, is devoted to analysis of the evidence.

However, the Edomites appear to have been opportunists, switching sides whenever it seemed advantageous. According to Jer 27:1 – 11, as recently as 594 – 593 BC the Edomites had been part of an international coalition including Moab, Bene Ammon, Tyre, and Sidon, which sent emissaries to Jerusalem to get Zedekiah to join them in rebelling against Nebuchadnezzar. However, when Tyre, Bene Ammon, and Judah launched the rebellion, Edom apparently listened to Jeremiah's counsel and withdrew from the alliance. By withdrawing, Edom secured its own existence and apparently received permission from Babylon to expand its territory in the Negev.

These data provide us with the terminus a quo of Obadiah's prophetic ministry. What about the terminus ad quem (latest possible date)? The oracles preserved in this short book obviously assume that Edom still exists as a nation and represents a significant threat to what remains of the Jewish community in Judah. This suggests they were delivered prior to Edom's fall. We lack clear and unequivocal evidence for this event, but a likely scenario is offered by the Chronicles of Nabonidus, a successor to Nebuchadnezzar, who ruled in Babylon from 556 – 539 BC. The chronicle recording his activities in this region in 553 BC, his third year, reads as follows:

> [The third (?) year, in the] month of Ab, [he marched] on the Ammanānum [and …] the orchards, fruits, as many as there were, […] among them, [he brought] to Babylon. [. ?. . The king be]came ill but recovered. In the month of Kislev, the king [mustered] his army […] and to Nabû-tattan-usur […] of Amurru to […] they set up their quarters [facing E]dom […] and the numerous troops [… ga]teway of Sintīni […] he killed him [… the tr]oops […].[22]

Although the dating is not certain, evidence for destruction prior to the Persian period has been found at Buseira (Bozrah), Tawilan, and Tell el-Kheleifeh.[23] This region continued to be occupied in the Persian period, but Edom's political and national status had been crushed, opening the doors to Nabatean Arabs to move in and take control. Accordingly, we may see in Nabonidus' campaign the fulfillment of Obadiah's prophecies.[24]

Obadiah's Rhetorical Aims and Strategy

Unlike kings or elders or even priests, prophets wielded no political power. Indeed, although false prophets often functioned as lackeys of the royal court,[25] the divinely authenticated prophetic institution in Israel exhibited an ad hoc flavor.

---

22. As translated by Jean-Jacques Glassner, *Mesopotamian Chronicles* (SBLWAW 19; Atlanta: Society of Biblical Literature, 2004), 235.

23. See Bartlett, *Edom*, 157 – 59.

24. So also Raabe, *Obadiah*, 55.

25. See, e.g., the prophets of Ahab in 1 Kgs 22. On this text see Daniel I. Block, "What Has Delphi to Do with Samaria? Ambiguity and Delusion in Israelite Prophecy," in *Writing and Ancient Near Eastern Society: Papers in Honour of Alan R. Millard* (ed. P. Bienkowski, C. Mee, and E. Slater; New York/London: T&T Clark, 2005), 189 – 216.

Prophets were called and commissioned by YHWH to address particular circumstances and to declare to the people the mind of God in response to those circumstances. Lacking political power, prophets could not impose their wills on the people. They were preachers, emissaries from the divine court declaring to the people the will of God. They could not force the people to comply; all they could do was plead with them to turn from their evil ways and to renew their covenant commitments to YHWH and to their fellow citizens.

As preachers, the prophets were rhetoricians, which meant that their work always involved at least four elements: a rhetor, an audience, a message, and a strategy.

1. The Rhetor [Speaker]

Inasmuch as prophets generally declared their messages in the first person, on behalf of God, and often explicitly appealed to divine inspiration for their messages, the true Rhetor in a book like Obadiah is YHWH. In Obadiah this is reflected in the opening citation formula, "Thus says Adonay YHWH concerning Edom" (v. 1b), as well as the twofold occurrence of the signatory formula, "The declaration of YHWH" (vv. 4d, 8b), and the declaration formula, "for YHWH has spoken" (v. 18g).[26] Obadiah was YHWH's authorized human spokesman.

But what can we say about the human rhetor? Since this prophet is never mentioned elsewhere, we are dependent on the book itself for the answer. The heading identifies him simply as "Obadiah." But this is of little help for three reasons.

First, the expression itself is ambiguous. Does "Obadiah" function as a personal name or is it simply an epithet. As noted earlier, as a personal name it appears in two forms: עֹבַדְיָהוּ and עֹבַדְיָה. Both consist of a verbal element, עָבַד, "to serve," plus the divine name (theophore) *yhwh*, thus meaning "servant of YHWH."[27] It is tempting to view the expression as a reference to a singular example of the group identified collectively as "my/his/your servants the prophets."[28] This phrase distinguishes these prophets from false prophets, who claimed to speak for Yahweh but whom God himself disowned (Ezek 12:21 – 13:23). In these contexts "servant" (עֶבֶד) does not suggest a menial role, but represents an honorific designation for one specially appointed and commissioned by God.[29] In Jer 23:16 – 22 YHWH characterizes

---

26. On these formulas, see the commentary.

27. The abbreviated form of the name occurs with increasing frequency in the waning decades of Judah's existence as an independent state, and it continues in the exilic and postexilic periods. In addition to the reference to Zevit in n. 10 above, see Jeaneane D. Fowler, *Theophoric Personal Names in Ancient Hebrew: A Comparative Study* (JSOTSup 49; Sheffield: Sheffield Academic, 1988), 371.

28. Some interpret Malachi similarly; that is, as a generic expression meaning "my messenger" rather than a personal name. For "my servants the prophets," see 2 Kgs 9:7; 17:13; Jer

7:25; 26:5; 29:19; 35:15; 44:4; Ezek 38:17; Zech 1:6; for "his servants the prophets," see 2 Kgs 17:23; 21:10; 24:2; Jer 25:4; Dan 9:10; Amos 3:7; Rev 10:7; 22:6; for "your servants the prophets," see Ezra 9:11; Dan 9:6; Rev 11:18.

29. As is reflected in many seals of courtiers that archaeologists have discovered. See, e.g., the Edomite seal from Tell el-Kheleifeh inscribed, "belonging to Qawsanal, servant of the king" (לקוסענל עבד המלך; Bartlett, Edom, 214); and "belonging to Shema servant of Jeroboam" (לשמע עבד ירבעם) from Megiddo (see Mordechai Cogan and Hayim Tadmor, *II Kings: A New Translation with Introduction and Commentary* (AB 11;

true prophets as those who stand in his council (סוד). Such was this "servant of YHWH."[30]

Even so it is preferable to interpret Obadiah as a personal name of an individual prophet. In the first instance, this name was common in ancient Israel, being ascribed to thirteen individuals in the OT[31] and attested frequently in Hebrew seals and inscriptions.[32]

Second, this form of name involving the root "servant" (עבד) plus a divine name was common throughout the ANE.[33]

Third, unlike the headings to most prophetic books, the present heading tells us nothing more about the prophet than his name.[34] Although the book of Jonah opens by introducing the main character in a narrative, most prophetic books open by naming the prophet responsible for what follows.[35] Whereas other headings offer information on the prophet's place in a family tree,[36] place of origin,[37] prior occupation,[38] or current profession,[39] the opening statement in Obadiah tells us nothing of the prophet's lineage, hometown, or occupation. Nor does it identify his current profession. The absence of information may suggest either that the person responsible for the book in its present form wanted to downplay the role of the human agent and highlight YHWH's role, or that this prophet was so well-known to the community

New York: Doubleday, 1988), 12a; and remarkably "belonging to Obadiah servant of the king" (לעבדיהו עבד המלך) unprovenanced (John C. L. Gibson, *Textbook of Syrian Semitic Inscriptions*, vol. 1, *Hebrew and Moabite Inscriptions* [Oxford: Clarendon, 1971], 62, 64. Only important officials had their own seals.

30. The epithet is also used of others engaged in divine service: Abraham, Moses, Joshua, David. In the NT, next to "apostle of Jesus Christ," "servant of Christ Jesus" was Paul's favorite self-designation (Rom 1:1; Gal 1:10; Phil 1:1; cf. Col 4:12; 2 Tim 2:24), though the title was also claimed by James (Jas 1:1), Peter (2 Pet 1:1), and Jude (Jude 1:1), and is attributed to those who serve God enthroned and the Lamb in Rev 22:3., etc.

31. In addition to the present prophet: (1) the steward in Ahab's court (1 Kgs 18:3–16); (2) a descendant of David (1 Chr 3:21); (3) a chief of the tribe of Issachar in Moses' time (1 Chr 7:3); (4) a member of Saul's family (1 Chr 8:38; 9:44); (5) a Levite descended from Jeduthun (1 Chr 9:16), perhaps a variant of Abda (Neh 11:17); (6) a warrior in David's troops from the tribe of Gad (1 Chr 12:9); (7) a Zebulunite, father of the chief Ishmaiah (1 Chr 27:19); (8) a prince commissioned by Jehoshaphat to teach the Torah in Judah (2 Chr 17:7); (9) a Levite from the line of Merari who supervised the refurbishing of the temple under Josiah (2 Chr 34:12); (10) a priest who accompanied Ezra from Babylon to Jerusalem (Ezra 8:9); possibly the same man who participated in the covenant ceremony

under Nehemiah (Neh 10:5); (11) a gatekeeper during Nehemiah's time (Neh 12:25).

32. See Dobbs-Allsopp et al., *Hebrew Inscriptions*, 611–12.

33. For Ugaritic, see F. Gröndahl, *Die Personennamen der Texte aus Ugarit* (Studia Pohl 1; Rome: Biblical Institute, 1967), 104–6; Punic and Phoenician, F. L. Benz, *Personal Names in Phoenician and Punic Inscriptions* (Studia Pohl 8; Rome: Biblical Institute, 1972), 369–72; Edomite, Bartlett, *Edom*, 203, 205–6; 211; Ammonite, W. E. Aufrecht, *A Corpus of Ammonite Inscriptions* (Ancient Near Eastern Texts and Studies 4; Lewiston: Mellen, 1989), 371; Aramaic and Canaanite, S. C. Layton, *Archaic Features of Canaanite Personal Names in the Hebrew Bible* (HSM 47; Atlanta: Scholars, 1990), 122, 130–31. To these we should add Old Arabic, Akkadian, and Amorite names involving *[w]ardu*, their word for "servant." Cf. *CAD 1/II*, 250.

34. Habakkuk and Malachi are equally cryptic.

35. This applies also to the book of Jeremiah, even though much of the book involves biographical narratives rather than prophetic utterances.

36. Isa 1:1; Jer 1:1; Ezek 1:3; Hos 1:1; Joel 1:1; Zeph 1:1; Zech 1:1.

37. Jer 1:1; Amos 1:1; Mic 1:1; Nah 1:1.

38. Jer 1:1 (priest); Ezek 1:3 (priest); Amos 1:1 (shepherd).

39. Hab 1:1 (prophet); Hag 1:1 (prophet); Zech 1:1 (prophet).

for which the book was produced that he did not need to be identified further. Remarkably, the editor classifies his work; it is a vision (חָזוֹן; cf. also Isa 1:1; Nah 1:1).[40]

2. The Audience

The opening citation formula ends with the word לֶאֱדוֹם, which could be translated "concerning Edom," "to Edom," or "for Edom." Assuming that these messages were never actually intended for Edom, most English translations choose the first option. However, this interpretation is unlikely on two counts. First, in the overwhelming number of cases involving the citation formula followed by the preposition לְ + a name or common noun, the preposition introduces the indirect object of the verb, that is, the addressee of the divine speech.[41] Second, here and in most instances elsewhere, the divine speech following the formula uses the second person of direct address.[42] In the present case the formula is separated from the divine speech, which begins in v. 2a, by the remainder of v. 1. Although all recognize that vv. 16–21 were intended for Judahite ears, from the opening formula some conclude that vv. 1–15 were actually intended to influence the Edomites. Obadiah's emphasis on Esau as Jacob's brother and his expression of horror at the way the Edomites have treated their relatives would have had the greatest rhetorical force if these utterances were actually addressed to Edom. Whether or not Obadiah ever faced the Edomites, since they were encroaching on Judahite territory and many were actually living on Judah's doorsteps in the Negeb, his messages could have found their way to Edomite territory.[43]

However, as in cases of inanimate addressees,[44] and especially in the oracles against foreign nations[45] — with the notable exception of Jonah, who actually went to Nineveh — we need to recognize two addressees, the hypothetical addressee, identified at the head of the prophecy, and the real addressee, the audience of the prophet. The issue is illustrated most dramatically in Ezekiel's oracles against the nations, particularly his oracles against Bene Ammon (Ezek 25:1–5) and Sidon (28:20–23), which open with the hostile orientation formula (lit.), "Son of man, direct your face toward …" (שִׂים פָּנֶיךָ אֶל/עַל). In these cases it is conceivable that Ezekiel physically turned his body so that he was facing the hypothetical addressee, but the utterance that followed was intended for the exiles before him. However, Obadiah spoke of

---

40. On which see further below.

41. Isa 45:1; 49:7; Jer 4:3; 29:4; Ezek 6:3; 7:2; 16:3; 26:15; 36:4; 37:5; Amos 5:4; 2 Chr 20:15. The only exceptions are found in Jer 14:10 and Ezek 12:19, where the sense "concerning" is confirmed by references to the parties named in the third person.

42. See Jer 49:7–22. Rather than casting Edom as the indirect object of the verb for divine speech, the superscription reads, לֶאֱדוֹם כֹּה אָמַר יהוה צְבָאוֹת, "Concerning Edom: Thus says YHWH Sebaoth." Except for vv. 14–16, which are cast in a heightened prose, if not poetry, the entire oracle speaks of Edom in the third person.

43. Thus Raabe, *Obadiah*, 57.

44. E.g., the mountains and valleys of Israel, Ezek 6:3; 36:4; Tyre, Ezek 26:16.

45. Collections occur in Isa 13–19; Jer 46:1–51:58; Ezek 25–32, 35, 38–39; Amos 1:3–2:5.

the grammatical addressee; the audience he sought to influence was his own fellow Judahites.

But what can we say about this audience? Some have suggested that the book of Obadiah was composed as a liturgical piece to be read and recited like a cantata.[46] However, if it was intended for formal use in worship, it seems odd that the version adopted for the canonical Book of the Twelve should have been the corrupted version.[47] Furthermore, the suggestion that the book was composed for recitation at some festival — perhaps the New Year's festival — is highly speculative. We know nothing of the festivals observed by the remnant of Judahites that survived the devastation of 586 BC and tried to eke out a living in the ruins of Jerusalem. It is difficult to imagine how any festivals would have been celebrated in this depressing context, without altar and temple.

Furthermore, since we have no certain evidence for a New Year's festival in the tabernacle ritual or in First Temple worship,[48] or even in Second Temple worship, it is doubtful this small and depressed band of survivors would have developed festivals celebrating the kingship of YHWH. For all they knew, far from being enthroned in the heavens, YHWH had actually abdicated and given way to the gods of the invaders. The spiritual condition of the people in Jerusalem suggested by Ezekiel (who provides us with the best clues available) renders it unlikely that Obadiah's prophecy might have been composed for such a positive event.

To answer the question of Obadiah's audience and context we must reflect more closely on the political, emotional, and spiritual state of the people whom Obadiah identifies as "the house of Jacob" (vv. 17c, 18a; cf. v. 10b). In the aftermath of the calamity of 586 BC, members of this "household" were found in four geographic contexts. The "house of Joseph" in v. 18b is shorthand for the northern kingdom of Israel, which, since 931 BC had been led by the tribe of Ephraim, and since the Omrides and their successors had ruled from Samaria (cf. v. 19c). However, with two decisive invasions in 732 and 722 BC the Assyrians had put an end to this nation, scattering the population that remained throughout the Assyrian empire and bringing in foreigners to fill the vacuum in the land (2 Kgs 17). In effect, the people of the northern kingdom had disappeared from history.

In the wake of the Babylonian conquest of Judah in 586 BC, the population that survived was distributed in three principal locations: Judah, Egypt, and Babylon. According to 2 Kgs 24:10–18, in response to Jehoiachin's resistance to Babylonian rule in 597 BC, Nebuchadnezzar had deported to Babylon the cream of the population — those with political and economic power — leaving behind the poorest of the land and installing Zedekiah, Jehoiachin's uncle, as vassal king. When Jerusalem

46. John D. W. Watts, *Obadiah: A Critical Exegetical Commentary* (Grand Rapids: Eerdmans, 1969), 24–27; idem, "Obadiah," *ISBE* (rev. ed.), 3:574–75.

47. For Watts' rearrangement of lines to smooth out the text, see further below.

48. See Daniel I. Block, "New Year," *ISBE* (rev. ed.), 3:529–32.

was razed a decade later, many who survived were deported as well, which left even fewer of the poorest of the population to eke out a living from the land (25:8 – 12).

Many questions concerning the exilic social scene remain, but certain features may be pieced together. First, although Jehoiachin lasted on the throne of David only three months, after the initial humiliation of deportation, he seems to have fared relatively well in Babylon. Babylonian inscriptions referring to him as "the king of the land of Judah" report that he and his sons received rations from the royal store-houses.[49] Whether this was favorable treatment for good behavior, a tactic to keep the pressure on Zedekiah back home, or treatment common for all foreign kings re-siding in Babylon is unclear. In any case, despite Jeremiah's pronouncements against Jehoiachin (Coniah, elsewhere also Jeconiah) in Jer 22:24, the prophets never lost hope in the Davidic line, and Jehoiachin remained the critical link.[50]

While Ps 137 locates the Judean exiles generally "by the rivers of Babylon," Eze-kiel's ministry focused on one specific community in Tel Abib, by the Chebar Canal.[51] This Chebar conduit was but one of many branches of an elaborate canal system that distributed water from the Tigris and the Euphrates throughout the city and its en-virons.[52] Although humiliated by the experience of deportation, economically the exiles appear to have recovered quickly. Indeed, they seem to have flourished, so that when Cyrus issued his decree in 539 BC permitting the Judeans to return to Jerusa-lem, many preferred not to go. Even though the Judean exiles integrated quickly into the Babylonian economy, they managed to remain a distinct ethnic and social com-munity, with their own elders and their own system of family records (Ezra 2; Neh 1). Without temple or altar, they also managed to preserve some Israelite religious institutions like circumcision and the Sabbaths (cf. Isa 56:2 – 4; 58:13; Ezek 44 – 46). Nevertheless, the prophecies of Ezekiel suggest that they brought all their apostatiz-

---

49. *ANET*, 308. For fuller discussion of Jehoiachin, espe-cially in the book of Ezekiel, see Daniel I. Block, "The Tender Cedar Sprig: Ezekiel on Jehoiachin," *Journal of Hebrew Bible and Ancient Israel* 2 (2012): 1 – 30.

50. Jer 23:5 – 6; Ezek 34:23 – 24; 37:24; Hag 2:23; Zech 4:6 – 9; 6:9 – 15.

51. נְהַר כְּבָר is the Hebrew equivalent of Akkadian *nār kabari/u*, "Kabaru canal," referred to occasionally in the fifth century BC archives of the Murashu family of bankers in Baby-lon. The designation *nār kabari* applied to at least three differ-ent canals. See R. Zadok, "Notes on Syro-Palestinian History, Toponomy and Anthroponymy," *UF* 28 (1996): 727. Whereas in the past scholars have located *nār kabari* near Nippur, some 80 km. southeast of Babylon (Block, *Ezekiel Chapters 1 – 24*, 84), the discovery of a cache of tablets near Borsippa next door to Babylon, some dating to the time of Ezekiel, and which iden-tify a place as "the city of Judah," (al-Yahdah; URU*ia-a-ḫu-du*) raise the possibility that Tel Abib may actually have been much closer to Babylon than previously thought. Three tablets have

already been published by F. Joannes and A. Lemaire, "Trois tablettes cunéiformes onomastique ouest-sémitique," *Tran-seuphratène* 17 (1999): 17 – 34. For a preliminary report of the remainder see L. E. Pearce, "New Evidence for Judaeans in Babylonia," *Judah and the Judeans in the Persian Period* (eds. O. Lipschits and M. Oeming; Winona Lake, IN: Eisenbrauns, 2006), 399 – 411. While this new evidence is tantalizing, Eze-kiel's Chebar probably ran through a suburb east of Nippur, within sight of the ziggurat of Enlil, which had for centuries been the hub of Mesopotamian religion. Thus D. L. Petter, *The Book of Ezekiel and Mesopotamian City Laments* (OBO 246; Fribourg: Academic Press, 2011), 110 – 11, based on research by D. R. Frayne communicated personally.

52. On the subject see R. Zadok, "The Nippur Region dur-ing the Late Assyrian, Chaldean and Achaemenian Periods Chiefly According to Written Sources," *IOS* 8 (1978): 266 – 332, esp. p. 287; E. Vogt, "Der Nehar Kebar: Ez 1," *Bib* 39 (1958): 211 – 16.

ing baggage with them, including their tendencies toward idolatry and all kinds of social evils (Ezek 18).

Some Judaeans were also living in colonies in Egypt. Jeremiah 44:1 locates Jewish settlements in Lower (Migdol, Tahpanhes, and Memphis) and Upper Egypt (Pathros). However, thanks to the discovery of numerous papyri, the best-known residence for Jews is the military colony on the island of Elephantine on the Nile. How these people got there is unknown; some may have arrived as early as the time of Manasseh. While these papyri reveal relative autonomy in internal social affairs, the religious climate was syncretistic. The Passover and Sabbaths were celebrated to YHWH, and a temple was built for him, but many other deities were also invoked: Eshem Beth-El, Anath Beth-El, Sati, Nebo, Anathyahu, Knubh,[53] which probably explains why the Egyptian Jews were largely irrelevant in later history.

Archaeological excavations and explorations confirm the complete devastation of the land of Judah in 586 BC, particularly the major population centers like Jerusalem and Lachish. In general, the people that remained suffered from severe depression, expressed in economic poverty, political lethargy, and spiritual numbness. Inevitably a new class of *nouvelle noblesse* (relatively) emerged, but with the same proclivity toward arrogance and spiritual turpitude as their predecessors. According to Ezek 11:14 – 16, they had no understanding of their rich religious heritage and no sensitivity or pity for their deported country folk. Like the exiles in Babylon, in truth the residents of Jerusalem and environs suffered from intense theological shock. Even though the prophets had justifiably denounced the people of Judah for their idolatrous and socially criminal ways, throughout the Babylonian crisis the people had maintained confidence in YHWH's obligation to rescue them. In keeping with standard ANE perspectives, this sense of security was based on the conviction of an inseparable bond among national patron deity (YHWH), territory (land of Canaan), and people (nation of Israel), as illustrated in the following "indestructible" triangle, with Deity (YHWH), Nation (Israel), and Land (Canaan) at the apexes (Fig. 1.1).

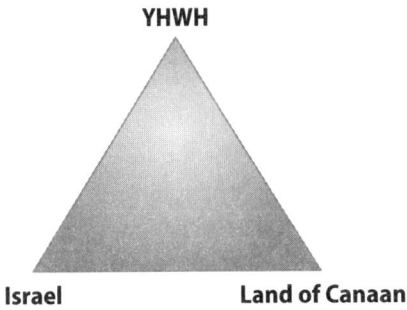

Figure 1.1: The Covenantal Triangle

---

53. *ANET*, 491 – 92.

More specifically, Israelite confidence in YHWH was founded on an official orthodoxy that rested on four immutable propositions, four pillars of divine promise: YHWH's irrevocable and eternal entitlement of Abraham and his descendants to the land of Canaan, YHWH's irrevocability and eternal covenant with Israel (Sinai), YHWH's irrevocable and eternal covenant with David, and YHWH's irrevocable and eternal commitment to Jerusalem/Zion as his earthly residence (Fig. 1.2). The nearer Nebuchadnezzar's forces came, the more the people clung to the promises of God.

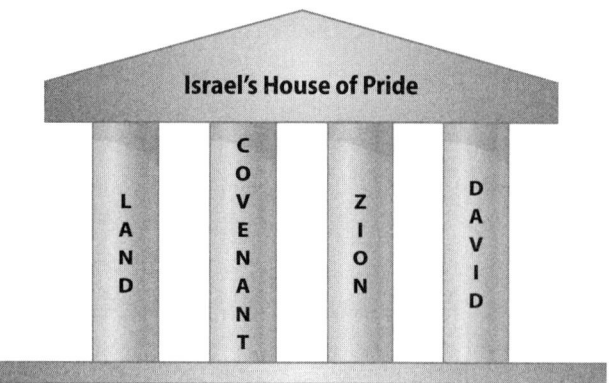

Figure 1.2: The Foundations of Israel's Security

But Jerusalem fell, the Davidic house was cut off, the temple was razed, and the major portion of the population was exiled from the land. For the survivors the spiritual fallout was more difficult to deal with than the physical distress. Nebuchadnezzar's victory had left them emotionally devastated, raising many questions about YHWH — questions of divine impotence, betrayal, and abandonment. Based on appearances, Marduk, the god of Babylon, had prevailed.

Far away in Babylon Ezekiel faced an audience that was equally disillusioned, cynical, bitter, and angry (Ezek 33:30 – 33). But his prophecies offer hints that similar attitudes prevailed back in Jerusalem. According to his first temple vision, prior to the fall of Jerusalem the people at home had introduced all kinds of abominable objects and practices to the temple compound itself (Ezek 8:1 – 18), and they filled the land with bloody crimes and the city with injustice (9:9; 11:6). They did so with cynical justification, "YHWH does not see us; YHWH has forsaken his land" (8:12; cf. 9:9), and a false sense of security within the city (11:3). Smugly claiming their presence in the land as a mark of YHWH's favor, they seized the property of their exiled countrymen, whose deportation they interpreted as a sign of final divine rejection (11:15 – 16).

These attitudes seemed to harden after the fall of Jerusalem. The meager survivors in the land continued their evil ways while claiming YHWH's promise to Abraham as their base of security (Ezek 33:23 – 29). Ezekiel's response was to declare that

Israel's future — which was securely grounded in YHWH's immutable commitments — rested with the exiles, not with the people back home. YHWH would bring them back, transform them from the inside out, and reconstitute them as his covenant community.[54] Meanwhile he had written off the people in the land.

If we assume Obadiah prophesied in Jerusalem, this was the audience he faced. Inasmuch as vv. 16 – 21 offer hope to his hearers, either this prophet's perception of the population of Jerusalem and environs differed fundamentally from his exiled colleague, or he spoke over his immediate audience's heads to the remnants of Israel scattered abroad. The prominence of references to the remnant (פְּלֵיטָה, v. 17a), exile (גָּלוּת, v. 20a, 20c), and the [dis]possession (יָרַשׁ, vv. 17c – 20b) of land suggest the latter. As in Ezekiel's and Jeremiah's restoration oracles, Obadiah's rhetorical aim was to rebuild his audience's hope in the eternal promises of God.

3. The Message

Responding to the spiritual and theological crisis created by the disaster of 586 BC, Obadiah sought to rekindle hope in his countrymen with two principal points. First, *divine justice will prevail* with respect to Israel's kinsmen the Edomites, who had gloated over Judah's fall. YHWH has not been blind to this filial betrayal; as they have treated the people of Judah, so they will be treated. Second, *divine fidelity will prevail* with respect to the descendants of Jacob themselves, presently dispersed among the nations and divorced from their homeland. YHWH had not forgotten his covenant with his people or his promises to the ancestors.

4. The Rhetorical Strategy

An old proverb says, "Good things come in small packages." This is certainly true of the book of Obadiah. Despite its brevity, the book presents a host of interpretive challenges, which led Jerome to comment in AD 396, "It is as difficult as it is brief."[55] However, rather than viewing the hermeneutical issues the book raises as distractions, we should consider them as intentional elements of his rhetoric. Several features stand out.

First, Obadiah adopts a style that is rhetorically emphatic and transparently passionate. Although in our Hebrew texts Obad 1 – 18 is laid out as poetry and vv. 19 – 21 are formatted as prose, most English translations cast the entire book as poetry.[56] This distinction may or may not be justified by observing the frequency of typical prose expressions and particles in the two sections. The sign of the definite

---

54. Ezek 11:17 – 21; 34:1 – 31; 36:22 – 38; 37:1 – 28.

55. *Quanto brevius est, tanto difficilius*, in his commentary on Obadiah (Abdias), PL 25,1578, accessible at http://www .documentacatholicaomnia.eu/02m/0347 – 0420,_Hieronymus,_Commentariorum _In_Abdiam_Prophetam_Liber_ Unus,_MLT.pdf.

56. Raabe is inconsistent. On the one hand, he declares the formatting of *BHS* to be correct (*Obadiah*, 6), but on the other hand, in his own translation (p. xxvi) he formats the entire text as poetry.

direct object, *'et*, occurs only twice in the first section (vv. 14b, 17c), but seven times in the much shorter second section (vv. 19[5x], 20d, 21a). The subordinating conjunction אֲשֶׁר occurs twice in the first section (actually as כַּאֲשֶׁר (vv. 15b, 16a), but it also occurs twice in the shorter second section (v. 20b, 20c). The definite article, הַ-, occurs only once in vv. 1 – 18 (v. 16b; הַגּוֹיִם), and six times in vv. 19 – 21 (vv. 19[3x], 20[3x]). *Waw* consecutive forms occur eleven times in vv. 1 – 18,[57] and four times in vv. 19 – 21.[58]

Although Raabe observes a perceptible movement in the book from pure poetry (vv. 1 – 15), to slightly more prosaic poetry (vv. 16 – 18), to pure prose (vv. 19 – 21), he and many other recent commentators treat the entire book as if it were poetry from beginning to end, counting syllables and accents in predetermined lines, looking for parallelism in strophes, and noting the dramatic imagery in the book. However, the fact that nine characteristically prose features occur in vv. 1 – 18 and that parallelism occurs in vv. 19 – 21 as well casts doubt first on the division of the book into poetry and prose sections and second on the usefulness of treating even the first section as poetry. The lack of consistency in the results when scholars count syllables and accents reinforces these doubts.[59] Although poetry may exhibit reticence in the use of certain grammatical forms on the one hand, and the heightened use of imagery, parallelism, and terse and rhythmic lines on the other, we may also find all these features in prose texts. Recent studies indicate that Hebrew notions of poetry and prose actually reflect a literary and syntactical continuum, with the prophetic style of books like Obadiah falling somewhere in between (Fig. 1.3):

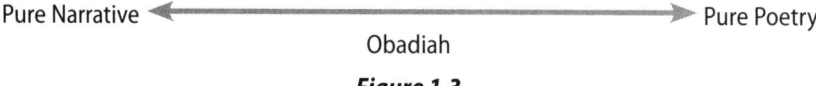

Figure 1.3

Prose and poetry are governed by the same rules of syntax and grammar. Both are dominated by the canonical ordering of clauses: the verb occurs in the initial position, followed by the subject or object or modifiers. Deviations from this pattern are more frequent in poetry, but these tend to occur in parallelism in the B-line.[60]

Despite being commonly formatted as poetry, Obadiah contains a host of additional features that compromise its poetic nature: prosaic references to the divine

---

57. All *wĕqāṭal* (וְקָטַל) forms referring to future events: vv. 8c (וְהַאֲבַדְתִּי); 9a (וְחַתּוּ); 10c (וְנִכְרַתָּה); 16c (וְשָׁתוּ וְלָעוּ); 16d (וְהָיוּ); 17b (וְהָיָה); 17c (וְיָרְשׁוּ); 18a (וְהָיָה); 18d-e (וְאָכְלוּ ... וְדָלְקוּ).

58. All *wĕqāṭal* (וְקָטַל) forms referring to future events: 19a, 19c (וְיָרְשׁוּ); cf. the normal *yiqṭōl* (יִקְטֹל) future form, יִרְשׁוּ, in 20d); 21a (וְעָלוּ); 21b (וְהָיְתָה).

59. Compare esp. Raabe, *Obadiah*, 9 – 14; Allen, *Joel, Obadiah, Jonah and Micah*, 146 – 68 (*passim*, next to his translation); Johan Renkema, *Obadiah* (Historical Commentary on the Old Testament; Leuven: Peeters, 2003), 45 – 73.

60. According to Nicholas Lunn, the canonical order is found in 85.5 percent of all narrative clauses and 66 percent of poetic clauses. For his summary, see *Word Order Variation in Biblical Hebrew Poetry: Differentiating Pragmatics and Poetics* (Paternoster Biblical Monographs; Eugene, OR: Wipf & Stock, 2006), 278 – 79. Excluding noun clauses, in Obadiah canonically ordered clauses account for 60 percent of the clauses, while noncanonical clauses account for 40 percent.

origin of Obadiah's utterances (vv. 1b, 4d, 8b, 18g); interjected phrases, clauses, and lines that break up parallelistic constructions and the flow of thought;[61] the deictic particle "See" (הִנֵּה, v. 2a); direct speech placed in the mouths of hypothetical characters (vv. 1e–f, 3e); while parallelistic in construction, prosaic grammar and syntax in the long series of accusations in vv. 12–14; the presence of long, complex sentences that resist reduction to parallel lines (vv. 9, 17c, 20a–d, 21a), and the imbalance between supposedly parallel lines (vv. 7a–b; 17a–b).

Viewed as a whole, the style of Obadiah is a far cry from the "pure" poetry we find in Hannah's song in 1 Sam 2:1–10 or in many of the psalms. If this is poetry, the word itself has lost all meaning. But neither is it smoothly flowing narrative or didactic prose, recounting events or coldly or logically presenting truth. Perhaps we do best to classify its style as a heightened form of rhetoric — impassioned speech that attempts to transform the minds and hearts of the audience, replacing cynicism and doubt with confidence and hope. While some (e.g., Ben Zvi) have rightly recognized that this short composition represents sophisticated literature, in the interjections especially we may recognize traces of the original oral prophetic event. Like the rest of the prophets, Obadiah was first and foremost a preacher. The literary style of the book testifies to his theological acumen, his understanding of rhetoric, and his passion for God.

Second, Obadiah intentionally appeals to higher authorities. Although he does not identify himself as a prophet, through his use of prophetic formulas in vv. 1b, 4d, 8b, and 18g he makes it clear that his message is not of his own design or merely wishful thinking. Since his message derives directly from YHWH, his audience must accept it as an expression of the divine disposition and the divine determination.

However, Obadiah did not only listen to the voice of God directly; he also heard it through intermediaries. In v. 1 he separates the divine citation formula from the cited text with a curious reference to a report from YHWH that "we have heard" through an "envoy [that] has been sent" (צִיר שֻׁלָּח). This message is not for Israel but for the nations, who are charged to engage Edom in war. But who is the messenger? The word for "envoy" (צִיר) could refer to a human messenger (as in Prov 13:17; Isa 18:2; 57:9). The sense of the word is confirmed in the first two texts by its association with "messenger" (מַלְאָךְ). However, since this envoy goes from YHWH to the nations, here and in Jer 49:14 this is best interpreted as a celestial angelic figure, presumably a member of the heavenly council.[62] In either case, both the nations and

---

61. Verse 1c–f separates the citation formula from the cited speech; v. 5c, "Ah, how you have been destroyed!" — separates the main clause from fronted subordinate clauses; v. 7e, "He has no clue!" is awkward after descriptions of the enemies' actions; v. 15b–d, "As you have done, it shall be done to you/Your action shall return on your own head," which most commentators link with vv. 1–14, rather than vv. 16–21. Critical scholars tend to interpret these interruptions as evidence of textual corruption or late editing.

62. So also Raabe, *Obadiah*, 114; Barton, *Joel and Obadiah*, 135–36.

Obadiah view the message as authoritative. While the former demonstrate this to be the case by responding to the command in v. 1e, "Rise up!" (קוּמוּ), with "Yes, let us rise against her for battle!" (v. 1f), the prophet does so by noting the message that he (and the people; "we") heard and by recording the nations' response.

But Obadiah has also heard the voice of YHWH through his professional predecessors. This short book offers a magnificent study in intertextuality, inasmuch as at least one half of the total involves adaptations of prior prophecies. The most obvious source is Jeremiah's oracle against Edom in Jer. 49:9 – 10c, 14 – 16, echoes of which are clearly heard in Obad 1 – 6, as the synopsis demonstrates on page 39.

Although it is possible that Jeremiah borrowed from Obadiah,[63] or that both derive from a common earlier oracle that circulated among the prophets,[64] most scholars who date Obadiah to the exilic period agree that Obadiah borrowed from Jeremiah.[65]

However, echoes of numerous other texts in the Hebrew Bible demonstrate that Obadiah had drunk deeply from Israel's traditions, both written and oral. The roots of the notion that Edomites consist not primarily of occupants of a land called Edom but of the descendants of Esau, and that Esau was the brother of the Israelites' ancestor Jacob, go back many centuries. In Deut 2 the population in the region of Mount Seir are identified as the "sons of Esau" (בְּנֵי־עֵשָׂו; vv. 4, 12, 22, 29). Like "sons of Israel" (בְּנֵי יִשְׂרָאֵל), in the Hebrew Bible this phrase perceives the population as a basically cohesive ethnic group, the descendants of a single ancestor. First, the narratives of Israel's ancestors include traditions of the personal life of the individual Esau, the brother of Jacob,[66] as well as an aetiological explanation for the identification of Esau with Edom (Gen 25:21 – 30). Second, reminiscences of the person Esau appear in later historical and prophetic texts (Josh 24:4; Mal 1:2 – 3). Third, Gen 36 provides a "national" genealogy outlining the early progress of the clan.[67] Accordingly, when Obadiah refers to the Edomites as "the house of Esau" (בֵּית עֵשָׂו; v. 18f) opposite "the house of Jacob" (בֵּית יַעֲקֹב; v. 18a) and "the house of Joseph" (בֵּית יוֹסֵף; v. 18b), he perceives them as a vast extended family.[68] The prophet reinforces this conviction by preferring the personal name Esau rather than Edom by a ratio of 7:2.[69]

Obadiah's oracles against Edom seem heavily indebted to other prophets who also railed against this nation. We have already noted the relationship between Obad

---

63. Thus, for example, Niehaus ("Obadiah," 501).

64. Cf. Douglas Stuart, *Hosea-Jonah* (WBC 31; Waco: Word, 1987), 414 – 15.

65. For discussion of the relationships among these texts, see commentary below.

66. Gen 25:19 – 34; 27:1 – 46; 28:5 – 9; 32:1 – 33:17; 35:1; 36:5 – 6.

67. Note the specific identification of Esau with Edom in vv. 1, 8, 9, 19, 43.

68. On the ethnic implications of the expression, "house of" + national name, see Daniel I. Block, "Israel's House: Reflections on the Use of בית ישראל in the Old Testament in the Light of Its Ancient Near Eastern Environment," *JETS* 28 (1985): 257 – 75.

69. "Edom" occurs in vv. 1b and 8c; Esau in vv. 6a, 8d, 9b, 18c, 18f, 19a, 21a. Vv. 8d, 9b, 19a, and 21a speak of "Mount Esau" or "Mount of Esau."

Obadiah	Jeremiah 49*	
1 The vision of Obadiah.		
Thus says Adonai YHWH	Concerning Edom,	7
concerning Edom — :	Thus says YHWH of Hosts — :	
A report we have heard from YHWH,	A report we have heard from YHWH,	14
and an envoy has been sent among the	and a messenger has been sent among the	
nations:	nations:	
	"Gather yourselves together	
	and come against her,	
Rise up! Yes, let us rise against her for battle!	and rise up for battle!"	
2 See,	Indeed see!	
small I will make you among the nations;	Small I will make you among the nations;	15
you are utterly despised.	despised among humankind.	
	The terror you inspire has deceived you —	
3 The smugness of your heart	the smugness of your heart;	16
has deceived you,		
the one who lives in the clefts of the rock,	the one who lives in the clefts of the rock,	
in your lofty dwelling,	you who hold the lofty hill.	
who says in his heart,		
Who will bring me down to earth?		
4 If you elevate . . . like an vulture,	Though you elevate your nest like an vulture,	
and if among the stars one sets your nest,		
from there I will bring you down —	from there I will bring you down —	
the declaration of YHWH.	the declaration of YHWH.	
5 If thieves came to you,	If grape gatherers came to you,	9
if burglars at night —	they will not leave gleanings.	
ah, how you have been destroyed! —	If thieves	
would they not steal enough for themselves?	at night —	
If grape gatherers came to you,	They pillage [only] what is enough for them.	
would they not leave gleanings?		
6 How Esau has been pillaged,	Indeed I have stripped Esau bare.	10
his storerooms ransacked!	I have uncovered his hiding places,	
	and he is not able to conceal himself.	

*What follows is my own translation of Jer 49:7, 9 – 10, 14 – 16, to reflect more precisely the links between these two texts.

1 – 6 and Jer 49, but prophecies specifically directed against Edom also occur in other collections of oracles against foreign nations.[70] Several features of Obadiah's prophecies suggest that he was familiar with some of these, and that he expected his hearers to be familiar with his quotations and allusions. The rhetorical questions, "Is it not that ..." (vv. 5d, 8a; הֲלוֹא)[71] and the exclamatory "How" (vv. 5c, 6a; אֵךְ) are intended to jog the audience's memory.[72] The Edomites' well-known history of mistreatment of Israelites underlies this and other oracles against Edom.

Beyond these major motifs, almost every verse contains an expression or motif that is encountered in other texts, most of which are earlier:[73]

1e-f	Divine call to rise for battle (Judg 18:9; Jer 6:4 – 6; cf. Hos 5:8; Mic 4:13; Jer 5:10)
2a-b	Making a nation/people insignificant among the nations (Mal 2:9)
3b-c	Seeking refuge/dwelling in the clefts of the cliffs (Song 2:14; Isa 2:21; Jer 16:16)
3e	Being brought down to earth (Jer 21:13; 49:4)
4a-b	Exalting [one's nest] like an vulture (Job 39:27)
5a-d	Thieves in the night (Job 24:14)
5e-f	Leave gleanings (Lev 23:22)
7a	Allies as "people of covenant" (Gen 14:13)
7c	Allies as "people of peace" (Ps 41:10[9]; Jer 38:22)
7d	Allies as those with whom one eats bread (Ps 41:10[9])
7e	Absence of understanding (Deut 32:28)
8c-d	Edom and wisdom (Jer 49:7; cf. 1 Kgs 4:30; Job 2:11)
9b	To cut off from Mount Esau/Seir by slaughter (Ezek 25:13; 35:7)
10a-b	Violence to your brother Jacob (Joel 4:19[3:19])
10c	Shame covering you (Jer 3:25; Mic 7:10)
11c	Enemies entering the gates of Jerusalem (Lam 4:12; Ezek 26:10)
11d	Casting lots for Jerusalem (Joel 4:3[3:3]; Nah 3:10)
12c-d	Rejoicing/opening the mouth wide over Judah's/Jerusalem's fall (Ps 35:19 – 21; Lam 2:16; 3:46; Ezek 35:13, 15)
12e – 14d	Defeat as a day of distress (2 Kgs 19:3; Isa 37:3; Zeph 1:15)
15a	The day of YHWH is near (Isa 13:6; Ezek 30:3; Joel 1:15; 2:1; 4:14[3:14]; Zeph 1:7, 14)
15b-c	As you have done, so it will be done to you (Judg 15:11; Jer 50:15, 29; Ezek 16:59; 35:11, 15)
15c	One's deeds returning on one's head (1 Kgs 2:32 – 33; Ps 7:17[16]; Ezek 16:43; Joel 4:4, 7[3:4, 7]; cf. Prov 12:14)

70. Isa 21:11 – 12; Ezek 25:12 – 14; 35; Amos 1:11 – 15; Mal 1:2 – 5.

71. In the translation accompanying the commentary below the word is rendered as "Would they not ...?" and "Will I not ...," respectively.

72. Cf. Amos 9:7b; Mic 3:1b, 11b; Hab 1:12; Zech 7:7; etc.

73. Cf. the listing of motifs in Raabe, *Obadiah*, 32 – 33; Ernst Wendland, "Obadiah's 'Day': On the Rhetorical Influence of Textual Form and Intertextual Influence," *JTT* 8 (1996): 45 – 47.

16a-b Drinking the cup of divine wrath (Isa 51:17 – 23; Jer 25:15 – 29; 49:12; 51:7; Ezek 23:31 – 34; Hab 2:16)

16a Jerusalem as "my holy mountain" (Isa 11:9; 56:7; 57:13; 65:11, 25; 66:20; Ezek 20:40; Joel 2:1; 4:17[3:17]; Zeph 3:11)

17a Mount Zion as refuge for escapees (Joel 3:5[2:32])

17b Mount Zion as a holy place (Joel 4:17[3:17])

18a-b A people/nation becoming a fire/flame (Isa 10:17)

18c Being burned like straw (Exod 15:7; Isa 33:11; Nah 1:10)

18f No survivors in Edom/Esau (Num 24:19)

19a Land of Edom/Esau being dispossessed (Num 24:18; Amos 9:12)

20a Israel as YHWH's host (Exod 14:19 – 20)

21a Savior deliverers (Judg 3:9, 15)

21b Dominion belonging to YHWH (Ps 22:29[28]; 1 Chr 29:11; cf. Pss 47; 93 – 94; 96 – 99)

While the list of Obadiah's expressions and motifs echoing earlier texts and traditions is impressive, it does not exhaust the evidence of dependence. We should note especially that with his invectives against Edom, in accordance with Deut 30:7, Obadiah has pronounced on Israel's enemy the broad categories of curses with which YHWH had originally threatened his own people in Deut 28, should they persist in rebellion against him.[74] However, the same applies to his message of hope after judgment for Israel. This hope is based on the ancient promises that devastation and exile cannot be YHWH's last word. He will act with compassion and in fidelity to his ancient commitments and ultimately restore his people to himself and to their land (Lev 26:40 – 45; Deut 4:29 – 31; 30:1 – 10).

The formulaic language in some of these expressions may suggest that Obadiah was not merely borrowing motifs from his prophetic predecessors,[75] but that he was also incorporating stock expressions in circulation at the time. In any case, his heavy use of traditional language and motifs has a profound effect on the rhetorical force of the book. Although the book is permeated by conventional motifs and language, Obadiah casts his message in his own creative form. Nevertheless, he is not preoccupied with novelty; rather, to the literary force of his distinctive style he adds the weight of prophetic tradition. His application of some of these motifs to Edom is new, but he hopes his audience will grasp both the meaning and the force of his utterance.[76]

---

74. Decimation: Deut 28:62; cf. 4:27; Lev 26:22, 36; humiliation and degradation: Deut 28:25, 27, 43, 44. So also Stuart, *Hosea-Jonah*, 416 – 17.

75. The convention of borrowing from earlier texts did not end with Obadiah. Malachi 1:2 – 3 and 2:9 seem to have been dependent on Obadiah; some argue the same for the references to Joel, but it is uncertain that Obadiah antedates Joel.

76. Similarly Wendland, "Obadiah's 'Day,'" 47.

The Structure of Obadiah

Unlike some prophetic oracles, which flow smoothly and exhibit a clear structure, Obadiah is difficult to outline. Verse 1 obviously functions as an introduction, establishing the context of Obadiah's prophecy, and the rest of the book represents a collage of prophetic pronouncements. While it is clear that the prophecy proper consists of a major section devoted to the denouncement of Edom (vv. 1 – 14) and a shorter section is intended to build hope in Israel (vv. 16 – 21), even the boundary between these two sections is blurred. Does v. 15 belong with the preceding or with what follows? The first line looks like the beginning of a new section, but lines 15b and c seem to fit better with what precedes.

In establishing the structural boundaries we need to consider several factors. Based on form and content, Watts interprets Obadiah as a liturgical judgment speech organized as follows:[77]

A. The Superscription (v. 1a)
B. The Audition (v. 1b-f)
C. The First Announcement of Judgment (vv. 2 – 4)
D. The Second Announcement of Judgment (vv. 5 – 10)
E. The Indictment and Deprecation (vv. 11 – 14)
F. A Theological Explanation (vv. 15 – 16)
G. A Vision of Conditions to Follow (vv. 17 – 21)

The last section is further broken up into fragments consisting of vv. 17, 18, 19 – 20, and 21, respectively. While attractive, this interpretation depends on the rearrangement of problematic lines,[78] and it disregards the embedded discourse markers. Rather than rearranging these lines, we should interpret their awkwardness as serving intentional literary and rhetorical purposes; to smooth out the text is to neutralize its effect.[79]

There is no doubt that Obadiah's prophecy contains the elements of a legal case (indictment and sentence), which might lend support to those who interpret it in terms of a covenant lawsuit.[80] However, rather than beginning logically with the indictment, Obadiah declares Edom's fate (vv. 2 – 9), then he describes their crimes (vv. 10 – 14), and finally he announces the implications of the judgment of Edom for

77. Watts, *Obadiah*, 37 – 65; idem, "Obadiah," 574 – 75. The verse numbering is his.

78. The citation formula is moved from v. 1b (our numbering) to the end of v. 1 to head up the actual prophecy; the interjection in v. 5c is dropped to the end of v. 5; the signatory formula in v. 8b is dropped to the end of v. 10.

79. Cf. Ernst Wendland, "Obadiah's Vision of 'The Day of

the Lord': On the Importance of Rhetoric in the Biblical Text and in Bible Translation," *JTT* 7(1996): 68 – 70. Much of Wendland's discussion is included in Ernst Wendland, *Prophetic Rhetoric: Case Studies in Text Analysis and Translation* (n.p.: Xulon, 2009), 40 – 67.

80. Cf. Herbert B. Huffmon, "The Covenant Lawsuit in the Prophets," *JBL* 78 (1959): 285.

the nations (vv. 15 – 16) and for Israel (vv. 17, 19 – 21), with another declaration of Edom's fate (v. 18) inserted.

While each subunit is actually more complex than this scheme suggests and will be discussed in greater detail below, here we need to summarize the stylistic and textlinguistic reasons for these divisions. The entire unit is held together by the word "day" (יוֹם), which occurs twelve times.[81] In terms of proportion, by word count the center of gravity lies in the second part, the judgment of Esau on his day of doom (see Fig. 1.4).[82] However, based on the discourse markers, the prophecy reaches its climactic section in vv. 15 – 18, with v. 17 marking the absolute pinnacle (D.3.a.).

A. Introduction: Setting the Stage for the "Days" (v. 1). As noted earlier, this verse sets the stage for the book, announcing its genre, a "vision" (חֲזוֹן); identifying the speaker, Obadiah; declaring the source of the prophecy (citation formula); and surprisingly introducing an external messenger and his report.

B. The Judgment: Esau's Humiliation on His "Day" of Doom (vv. 2 – 10). The first section of the actual oracle is formally marked at the beginning by the deictic particle, "See" (הִנֵּה), in v. 2a, and at the end by the summary statement in v. 10. Although the opening clause of v. 10a appears to introduce the indictment, this clause is merely a summary statement, grounding the following two clauses, which represent the center of gravity in this verse, and bringing YHWH's announcement of Edom's doom to a climactic bi-cola closure.[83]

C. The Indictment: Esau's Crimes on the "Day of Jacob" (vv. 11 – 14). This section picks up on the summary indictment in v. 10 (Esau's violence to his brother) and unpacks it in penetrating detail. This is the most cohesive section of the book. It opens with a reference to a fateful day involving Esau — though not as the victim but as a criminal on someone else's day (v. 11). Although the word "day" is repeated another eight times in vv. 12 – 14, the focus has shifted to "Jacob's day" and Esau's response. He not only refused to stop those who razed Jerusalem, but he also joined in the violence against his own brother.

D. The Bad Good News: The Demise of Esau on the "Day of YHWH" (vv. 15 – 18). As in Ezekiel's oracles against the nations (Ezek 25 – 32), from Jacob's perspective this strophe represents good news: YHWH will dispose of Jacob's enemies. The new section is signaled by the particle *kî*. Most English translations render the word as "For," in which case v. 15 belongs with the preceding, presumably providing the grounds for the indictment of Esau.[84] However, this is both illogical and ungrammatical. First, the nearness of the day of YHWH cannot be the grounds for

---

81. Vv. 8a, 11a, 11b, 12a, 12b, 12d, 12f, 13b, 13d, 13f, 14d, 15a.

82. The vertical space assigned to each section is based on word count. The word counts in the respective sections are as follows: A, 17 words; B, 101 words; C, 65 words; D, 61 words;

E, 46 words; Total, 290 words.

83. So also Wendland, "Obadiah's 'Day,'" 31 – 32; idem, *Prophetic Rhetoric*, 43 – 44.

84. Thus ESV, NASB, NRSV; Raabe, *Obadiah*, xxv, 189 – 90.

Figure 1.4:

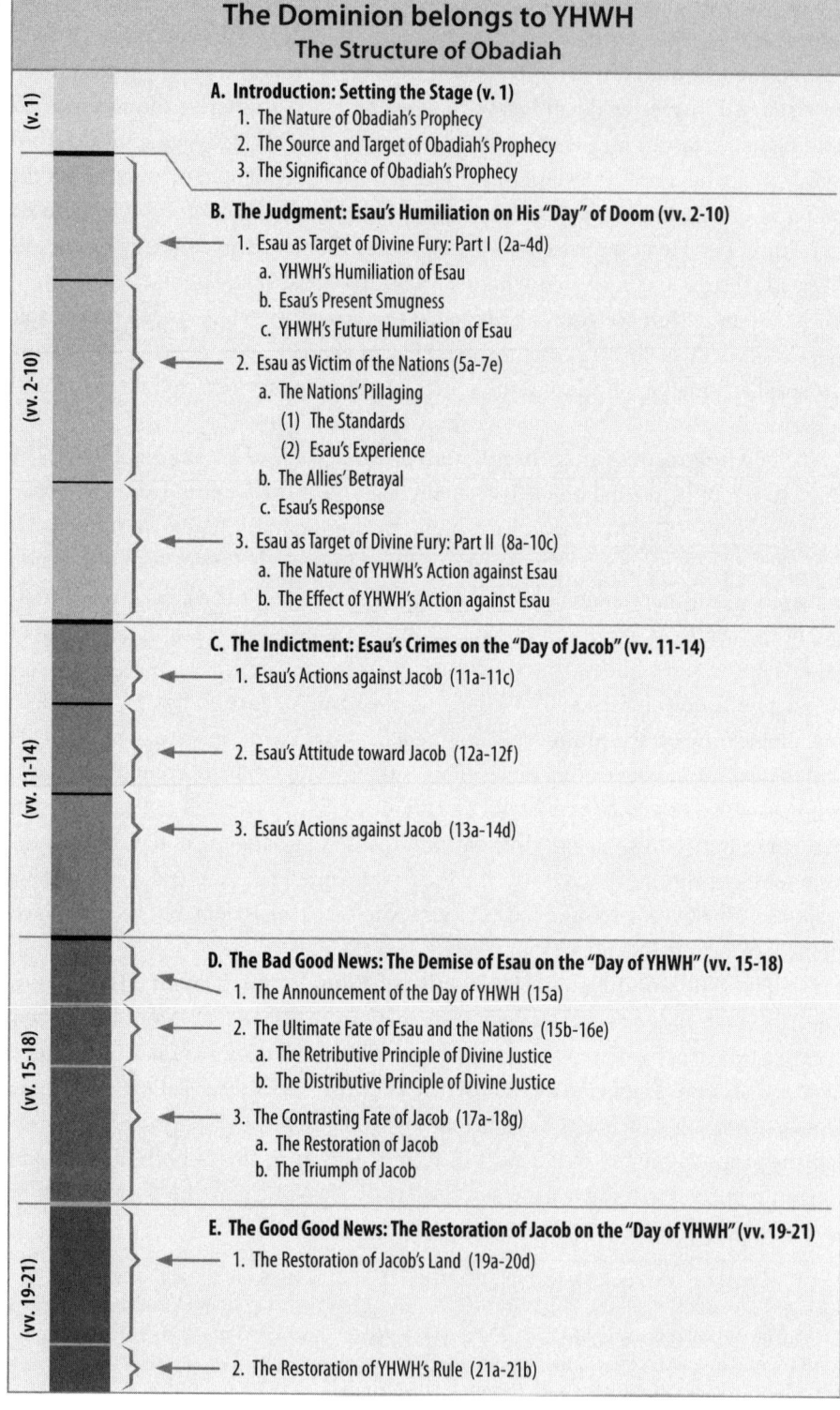

The Dominion belongs to YHWH
The Structure of Obadiah

(v. 1)

A. Introduction: Setting the Stage (v. 1)
    1. The Nature of Obadiah's Prophecy
    2. The Source and Target of Obadiah's Prophecy
    3. The Significance of Obadiah's Prophecy

B. The Judgment: Esau's Humiliation on His "Day" of Doom (vv. 2-10)
    1. Esau as Target of Divine Fury: Part I (2a-4d)
        a. YHWH's Humiliation of Esau
        b. Esau's Present Smugness
        c. YHWH's Future Humiliation of Esau
    2. Esau as Victim of the Nations (5a-7e)
        a. The Nations' Pillaging
            (1) The Standards
            (2) Esau's Experience
        b. The Allies' Betrayal
        c. Esau's Response
    3. Esau as Target of Divine Fury: Part II (8a-10c)
        a. The Nature of YHWH's Action against Esau
        b. The Effect of YHWH's Action against Esau

(vv. 2-10)

C. The Indictment: Esau's Crimes on the "Day of Jacob" (vv. 11-14)
    1. Esau's Actions against Jacob (11a-11c)
    2. Esau's Attitude toward Jacob (12a-12f)
    3. Esau's Actions against Jacob (13a-14d)

(vv. 11-14)

D. The Bad Good News: The Demise of Esau on the "Day of YHWH" (vv. 15-18)
    1. The Announcement of the Day of YHWH (15a)
    2. The Ultimate Fate of Esau and the Nations (15b-16e)
        a. The Retributive Principle of Divine Justice
        b. The Distributive Principle of Divine Justice
    3. The Contrasting Fate of Jacob (17a-18g)
        a. The Restoration of Jacob
        b. The Triumph of Jacob

(vv. 15-18)

E. The Good Good News: The Restoration of Jacob on the "Day of YHWH" (vv. 19-21)
    1. The Restoration of Jacob's Land (19a-20d)
    2. The Restoration of YHWH's Rule (21a-21b)

(vv. 19-21)

Edom's actions against Jacob as described in vv. 11 – 14. Second, if v. 15 is attached to the preceding, then v. 16 begins with the same particle. However, a new paragraph cannot begin with "because." Therefore, it is preferable to interpret the opening כִּי in v. 15a as an asseverative focus particle, "Surely, indeed!" shifting attention away from Jacob's day to the day of YHWH.[85] But the focus returns to Judah in v. 16, suggesting that the opening כִּי here should also be interpreted as a focus particle. Critical scholars generally transpose lines 15a and 15b-c, treating the former as the introduction to vv. 16 – 18 (or v. 21) and the latter as the conclusion to lines 10 – 14.[86] However, this changes the rhetoric significantly and obscures the relationship that Obadiah is trying to establish between Edom and the nations.

After the opening thesis statement (v. 15a) this paragraph is cast in four parts, exhibiting an a-b-c-a pattern, with the first and last segments involving the fate of Edom as an individual nation, the second and third involving Judah/Jerusalem; the paragraph highlights the contrast between their past experience of the fury of YHWH and the future experience of his grace. Edom is indeed the archetype of all nations that oppose YHWH and his people, but the discourse structure, involving successive focus particles in vv. 15 and 16, and the marked structure of v. 17a (MVS)[87] signal the climax of the entire book. In a remarkable turnaround, Jacob, who had previously suffered horrendously at the hands of the nations and under the wrath of YHWH, will be the beneficiary of YHWH's actions against the nations. This section closes with an epiphoric reference to no survivors (שָׂרִיד) — the same key word as in the last clause of v. 14 — and a final divine declaration formula: "for YHWH has spoken" (v. 18f-g).

E. The Good Good News: The Restoration of Jacob on the "Day of YHWH" (vv. 19 – 21). Here the focus shifts completely. Esau is still in the picture, being named at the beginning (v. 19a) and at the end (v. 21a), but only as the object of verbs rather than the subject. Furthermore, the issue is no longer the Edomites — that is, "the house of Esau" (v. 18c, f), Jacob's brother — but the land they occupied, awkwardly referred to as Mount Esau (as in vv. 8 – 9). This shift is probably not surprising, especially since Obadiah had declared in v. 18f that no one from the house of Esau would survive the judgment of YHWH. The key word in vv. 19 – 20 is "to possess" (יָרַשׁ), which occurs three times (vv. 19a, 19c, 20d), and is assumed in the other three elliptical clauses (vv. 19b, 20a, 20b). However, the subject throughout is either different parts of the land of Israel or the remnant of exiles who return to the land.

---

85. On the use of כִּי to mark a prominent juncture, see C. M. Follingstad, *Deictic Viewpoint in Biblical Hebrew Text: A Syntagmatic and Paradigmatic Analysis of the Particle* כי (Dallas: SIL, 2001), 52.

86. E.g., Hans Walter Wolff, *Obadiah and Jonah: A Commentary* (trans. M. Kohl; Minneapolis: Augsburg, 1986),

37 – 38; Allen, *Joel, Obadiah, Jonah and Micah*, 135 – 36, 159, n. 16. For defense of the received order, see the commentary below.

87. Modifier + verb + subject; as opposed to the canonical structure with the verb in the first position.

The book climaxes with a glorious declaration of righted wrongs and the triumph of divine compassion: Israel will rule over Mount Esau from Mount Zion, and YHWH will rule as king over all. We may summarize the plot of Obadiah diagrammatically as follows:

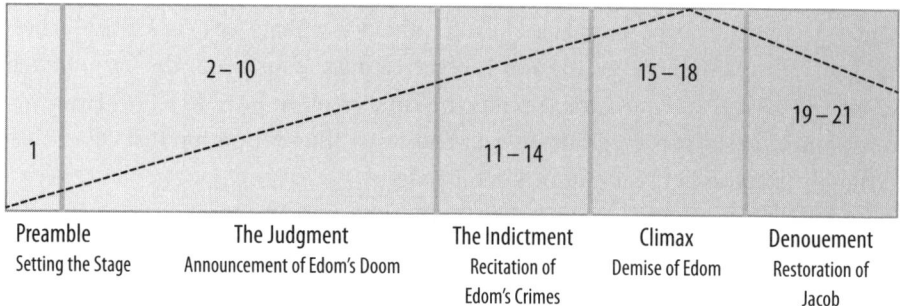

Preamble	The Judgment	The Indictment	Climax	Denouement
Setting the Stage	Announcement of Edom's Doom	Recitation of Edom's Crimes	Demise of Edom	Restoration of Jacob

World of Obadiah:

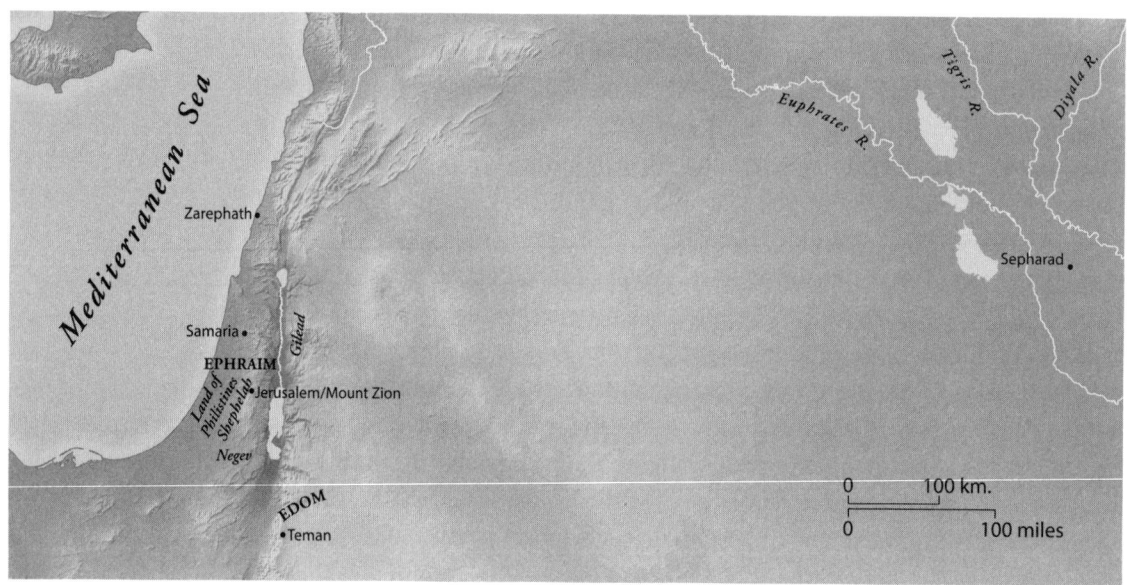

Obadiah 1

A. Introduction: *Setting the Stage for the "Days"*

Main Idea of the Passage

The first verse of Obadiah sets the stage for the book, identifying for readers and hearers the nature of Obadiah's prophecy (a vision), the source (YHWH) and target (Edom) of his prophecy, and the significance of his prophecy (the beginning of the end for Edom).

Literary Context

Like most prophetic books of the OT, Obadiah begins by introducing information that is critical to interpreting the book. The opening statement not only gives the identity of the human speaker, but through the citation formula identifies the divine voice behind the prophet. Accordingly, when we hear first person declarations (vv. 2a, 4c, 8c), we know they are not Obadiah's predictions of what he will do, but YHWH's own words.

Strictly speaking, YHWH's speech does not follow immediately after the citation formula, leading scholars either to delete the formula as a secondary addition[1] or to rearrange the text so that this formula comes immediately before v. 2a.[2] However, as we will see, Obadiah has a penchant for surprising readers and hearers with *apparently* misplaced clauses. These surprises keep the audience alert and contribute to the rhetorical force of the whole. At the same time, sometimes this formula functions as a code expression for authorized prophetic speech generally, and it may appear without a following divine address.[3] Its placement here reflects the fact that all true

---

1. A. Weiser, *Die Propheten Hosea, Amos, Obadja, Jona, Micha* (ATD 24: Göttingen: Vandenhoeck and Ruprecht, 1974), 208.

2. Thus Wolff, *Obadiah and Jonah*, 33, 45; Watts, *Obadiah*, 38, 46 – 47.

3. See Ezek 2:4. The signatory formula may also be used this way: Ezek 13:6 – 7. For another example of an unexpected lack of an anticipated divine word, see Amos 4:12.

prophetic speech is divine speech, and that all that follows comes under the rubric of true prophecy — even the report of a message delivered to someone other than the prophet. The enigmatic reference to a message sent among "the nations" (הַגּוֹיִם) inserts a motif that will become significant later, albeit in an ironic reversal of roles. Whereas this note presents the nations as the agents through whom YHWH will execute his judgments against Edom, later they will share Edom's fate as objects of YHWH's wrath (vv. 15a, 16).

> ➡ **A. Introduction: Setting the Stage for the "Days" (v. 1)**
> B. The Judgment: Esau's Humiliation on His "Day" of Doom (vv. 2 – 10)
> C. The Indictment: Esau's Crimes on the "Day of Jacob" (vv. 11 – 14)
> D. The Bad Good News: The Demise of Esau on the "Day of YHWH" (vv. 15 – 18)
> E. The Good Good News: The Restoration of Jacob on the "Day of YHWH" (vv. 19 – 21)

Translation and Exegetical Outline[4]

(See the next page.)

Structure and Literary Form

The introduction consists of three parts: a simple third person identification of the prophet responsible for the utterances in this book (v. 1a), the citation formula (v. 1b), and an enigmatic reference to a report of a communication event — complete with narrative preamble identifying the source of the message and the audience for whom it is intended (v. 1c-d), a citation of the message (v. 1e), and the audience's response (v. 1f). Syntactically the introduction is awkward; the three main parts are not linked by conjunctions of any sort and appear to be stand-alone fragments. The first line (v. 1a) functions as a superscription for the entire book, inviting us to hear[5] it as a unified whole. If the citation formula invites us to read the entire book as prophetic speech, then the report of a messenger going to the nations creates anticipation and provides a lens through which to read what follows. Yes, the nations will be involved in Edom's demise, but no, they will not be acting on their own; they will be fulfilling a divine command. This opening introduces us to four different voices: (a) the editor

---

4. In keeping with the purposes of this commentary series, my translation tends to be quite formal rather than idiomatic. Here and elsewhere the formatting of lines attempts as much as possible to reflect the discourse structure of the Hebrew text. Usually verbal expressions will call for a separate line. Syntacti-

cal subordination is marked by indented lines.

5. The Scriptures were largely written to be heard by the community rather than to be analyzed by academics — as we are doing in this commentary.

Obadiah 1

		A. Introduction: Setting the Stage (v. 1)
1a	חֲזוֹן עֹבַדְיָה	The vision of Obadiah. — 1. The Nature of Obadiah's Prophecy
1b	כֹּה־אָמַר אֲדֹנָי יְהוִה לֶאֱדוֹם	Thus says Adonai YHWH concerning Edom, — 2. The Source and Target of Obadiah's Prophecy
1c	שְׁמוּעָה שָׁמַעְנוּ מֵאֵת יְהוָה	A report we have heard from YHWH,
1d	וְצִיר בַּגּוֹיִם שֻׁלָּח	and an envoy has been sent among the nations: — 3. The Context of Obadiah's Prophecy
1e	קוּמוּ	Rise up!
1f	וְנָקוּמָה עָלֶיהָ לַמִּלְחָמָה׃	Yes, let us rise against her for battle!

of the book, who identifies the genre and the prophet; (b) the prophet, who begins with the citation formula; (c) heavenly envoys, who call on the nations to rise up against Edom — "Rise!" (קוּמוּ); (d) the nations, who declare their positive response: "Yes, let us rise against her for battle!"

Explanation of the Text

1. The Nature of Obadiah's Prophecy (v. 1a)

It is fitting that the shortest prophetic book should also have the shortest superscription. As noted earlier, the superscription offers no information on the prophet except his name. Meaning "servant of YHWH," Obadiah (עֹבַדְיָה) presents this man as a representative of prophets frequently referred to as "my/your/his servants the prophets."[6] We know nothing of this Obadiah's vocation, home, or family. Although the book is obviously the work of a man learned in Israel's scriptural and prophetic tradition, if our view of the context of the oracles in this book is correct, he probably came from the lower classes, since these were the people whom Nebuchadnezzar left behind when he deported the Judahite population in 598 BC (2 Kgs 25:14).

Whoever was responsible for the final shape of the book classified its contents as a "vision." The word חָזוֹן derives from a verb חָזָה, "to see," and is used especially of revelatory visions (Ezek 12:27; 13:16). It also occurs in the superscriptions of the books of Isaiah (Isa 1:1; cf. 2 Chr 32:32) and Nahum (Nah 1:1), and is applied to Habakkuk (Hab 2:2) as well. The latter two reflect how flexibly the word could be used. In Nah 1:1 "vision" is paired with "oracle, burden" (מַשָּׂא), and in Hab

2:1 the prophet climbs the watchtower to "see" (רָעָה) what YHWH will say to him in answer to the questions he raised in Hab 1. The Balaam narratives in Num 23 – 24 portray this prophet from Mesopotamia as one "whose eye is open," "who hears the words of God," and "who sees a vision [חָזָה מַחֲזֶה] of Shaddai" (24:3 – 4).[7] While YHWH often revealed prophetic messages in visionary form,[8] Obadiah leaves no hint of an optical revelatory event, suggesting that here חָזוֹן speaks not only of physical sight but of extraordinary perception. Inspired by YHWH, Obadiah is able to "see" the future of Edom and his own people and to paint a graphic verbal picture of that future.

2. The Source and Target of Obadiah's Prophecy (v. 1b)

The formula "Thus says Adonay YHWH"[9] highlights the speaker's heraldic role and the speech that follows as the very words of the one who sent him. This declaration is commonly referred to as the "messenger formula," because it usually introduces the utterance of a person who has been sent with official authority to speak on behalf of a superior.[10] However, since it can also be used in circumstances not involving an officially commis-

---

6. For references, see above, p. 28.

7. The same root is used of the prophet Balaam, "son of Beor," in the ninth-century BC text from Deir 'Alla in Jordan. Like this book, the Deir 'Alla text begins with a superscription: "The misfortunes of the Book (ספר) of Balaam, son of Beor. A divine seer (חזה) was he. The gods came to him at night and he beheld (ראה) a vision (מחזה) in accordance with El's utterance

(משׂא)." As translated by Baruch A. Levine, *COS* 2.27, p. 142.

8. Isa 6; Ezek 8 – 11; 37; 40 – 48; Amos 7 – 8.

9. כֹּה אָמַר אֲדֹנָי יהוה.

10. S. A. Meier, *Speaking of Speaking: Marking Direct Discourse in the Hebrew Bible* (VTSup 46; Leiden: Brill, 1992), 179 – 90.

sioned spokesman (cf., e.g., 1 Sam 9:9; 20:22), it is better designated as a "citation formula." Whether or not it functions as a messenger formula depends on the relationship between the ones who use the formula and the persons whose words they quote.

To understand how the formula functioned in relation to divine speech, we might look at a mundane example involving only humans. Conveniently, the narratives of Jacob and Esau in Genesis provide the best illustration. In Gen 32:4 – 7[3 – 6], with obvious fear Jacob prepares to meet Esau after his sojourn in Aram.

Preamble	**Identification of Commissioner**	Jacob sent messengers (מַלְאָכִים) ahead of him
	Addressee	to Esau his brother,
	Place	in the land of Seir, the country of Edom.
Commission	**Introduction**	And he commanded them, saying:
	The Charge	"Thus you shall say to my lord, Esau:
Message	**Citation Formula**	'Thus says your servant Jacob:
	Report	I have sojourned with Laban, and stayed there until now.
	Purpose	Now I possess oxen, donkeys and flocks, and male and female servants.
		And I have sent [messengers] to inform my lord
		so I might find favor in your sight.'"
Mission	**Return**	The messengers returned to Jacob saying:
Accomplished	**Report**	"We came to your brother Esau;
	Reaction	now he is coming out to meet you,
		accompanied by four hundred men."

Whereas these messengers here were "envoys" (מַלְאָכִים) of their master Jacob, prophets were envoys commissioned by God and authorized to speak for him with his voice — hence the use of the first person in prophetic speeches. As was the case with Jacob in commissioning this envoy, the goal of prophetic speech is rhetorical: to get the addressees to view reality the way the divine Commissioner perceives it and to change their conduct in accordance with that reality. This typically involves breaking down prevailing perceptions and reconstructing them according to the speaker's mind. The communication/rhetorical event involves five phases: (1) commissioning the messenger; (2) transmitting the message to the messenger; (3) delivering the message; (4) reporting the completion of the assignment; (5) the response of the addressee. The book of Obadiah reports only the second phase; we do not know the circumstances or means by which YHWH commissioned Obadiah, the manner or context in which he delivered his message, or the response of the addressees.

The text highlights the authority of the one sending Obadiah by identifying him as "Adonay YHWH" (אֲדֹנָי יהוה). That this should be the first of seven occurrences of the divine name YHWH (יהוה) scattered throughout the text sends an early signal of the central character in the book. Remarkably, four of these seven occur in formulaic expressions highlighting the divine authority of the words declared (vv. 1b, 4d, 8b, 18g); three portray him as the determining actor in the events described

(vv. 1c, 15a, 21b). The citation formula occurs in the OT with God as the sending authority more than 430 times: 293 involve the divine name without title, "Thus says YHWH"; 134 involve the compound form we have here; and a few more involve other epithets for God.[11]

Obadiah's present preference for the compound form may reflect the influence of Ezekiel, since the overwhelming majority of cases involving this form occur in that book (122/134), and Ezekiel uses the shorter form only three times (11:5; 21:8[3]; 30:6).[12] Whatever its inspiration, the addition of Adonay highlights YHWH's authority to govern the world as he deems right and to exercise his sovereign power in the judgment of the nations and the salvation of his people. The addition here creates a sensitive inclusio with the last statement of the book: "the dominion" (הַמְּלוּכָה) does indeed belong to YHWH (v. 21b).

The citation formula identifies the target audience as Edom, whose divinely assigned territory lay south of the Zered Brook, which flowed into the south end of the Dead Sea (Deut 2:1 – 7).[13] The OT often refers to the mountainous heartland of Edomite territory as "Seir." The Edomite genealogy preserved in Gen 36 suggests that this geographic designation for the land derived from the name of an ancestor of the Horites (36:20 – 30), whom the Edomites displaced (Deut 2:12). Edom emerged as a nation approximately the same time as Israel, though they never achieved Israel's political and economic power, and because they have left no literary records (like the OT), the history of this nation is obscure.[14]

Our concern here is not the political history of Edom, but the history of this people's relationship with Israel and their significance for the prophecy of Obadiah. The way the prophet refers to the Edomites is telling. It is appropriate that the heading to the book should identify the Edomites by their national name, "Edom." In the oracle itself this name occurs only once (v. 8c), where the parallelism demands a correlation with Mount Esau (v. 8d). Otherwise the prophet always refers to the Edomites by the simple name of their eponymous ancestor, "Esau" (v. 6a), or the collective designation, "house of Esau" (v. 18c, f),[15] and to their homeland as "Mount Esau" (vv. 8d, 9b, 19a, 21a), a designation for Mount Seir that occurs nowhere else.[16]

Obadiah's preference for the name Esau reflects his rhetorical concern. As noted, he is not interested in the political history of Edom or Edom's economic standing among the nations. To him Edom is a person, the brother of Jacob (vv. 10b, 12a), who shares a common ancestry in the first two patriarchs, Abraham and Isaac, but whose history of violence against his twin brother will finally be answered. According to biblical tradition, the history of conflict between Israel and Edom antedates their birth. Genesis 25:20 – 34 reports that Jacob and Esau were at odds already in their mother's womb. Remarkably, the patriarchal narratives actually paint Esau in a more positive light than Jacob, whose name means "cheat." In purchasing the birthright for a pot of lentil stew, Jacob was a shrewd opportunist, capitalizing on his brother's hunger (25:29 – 34); and when he stole the ances-

---

11. "God YHWH, who created the heavens" (הָאֵל; Isa 42:5); "God" (הָאֱלֹהִים; 2 Chr 24:20); "Adonay" (אֲדֹנָי; Isa 21:16; Ezek 21:14[9]).

12. It may also explain why Obadiah was placed after Amos, who uses the compound form of the name twice with this formula (Amos 3:11; 5:3) and an additional eighteen times.

13. See Beitzel, *Moody Atlas*, 33, 36 – 37.

14. For the most thorough study, see Bartlett, *Edom*; idem, "Edom," *ABD*, 2:287 – 95.

15. This is no different than referring to Israel as "Israel," or "household of Israel," rather than Canaanites, from the geographic name of the region west of the Jordan.

16. The sevenfold reference to Esau by personal name matches the seven references to the divine antagonist by name.

tral blessing, he acceded to his mother's deceitful schemes (27:1 – 45). Esau could not help it if he was hungry when he came in from the field, and it was not his fault if their father Isaac overrode YHWH's oracle (25:23) and sought to bless his eldest son before his death (27:7, 27 – 29). When Jacob returned from Haran, he was the one with the guilty conscience over what happened decades earlier (32:1 – 11), while Esau held no grudges (33:1 – 17).

The present oracle is a response, not to the individual Esau's abuse of Jacob, but the abuse the latter's descendants experienced at the hands of the descendants of the former. However, as we will see, Obadiah does not respond to centuries of abuse but to a particular recent moment in history.[17]

3. The Context of Obadiah's Prophecy (v. 1c-f)

The remainder of the introduction represents the first part of an extended statement (vv. 1b – 5f) inspired by Jeremiah's oracle against Edom in Jer 49:7 – 22.[18] Obadiah rearranges and adapts the material according to his own rhetorical agenda, but the echoes add the weight of prophetic tradition to his utterances. The present text derives from Jer 49:14. The relationship between these texts may be highlighted by juxtaposing literal translations as follows:

Jeremiah 49:14a-b	Obadiah 1c-f
A report I have heard from YHWH, and an envoy among the nations is sent: "Gather together and come against her, and rise up for the battle."	A report we have heard from YHWH, and an envoy has been sent among the nations: "Rise up!" "Yes, let us rise against her for battle!"
שְׁמוּעָה שָׁמַעְתִּי מֵאֵת יְהוָה וְצִיר בַּגּוֹיִם שָׁלוּחַ הִתְקַבְּצוּ וּבֹאוּ עָלֶיהָ וְקוּמוּ לַמִּלְחָמָה	שְׁמוּעָה שָׁמַעְנוּ מֵאֵת יְהוָה וְצִיר בַּגּוֹיִם שֻׁלָּח קוּמוּ וְנָקוּמָה עָלֶיהָ לַמִּלְחָמָה

Each line involves subtle but significant changes, which we will note as we proceed through Obadiah's utterance. Although both utterances are meaningful and both open with an alliterative clause, Obadiah's text certainly poses more interpretive challenges. Whereas Jeremiah's first line is autobiographical, Obadiah complicates matters by changing the singular verb to the plural. Who else is listening in on this communication from YHWH? Either this is an editorial "we," or Obadiah

---

17. In contrast to Amos, who knows of Edomite violence against and his stifling of brotherly compassion toward his brother in the eighth century BC (Amos 1:11 – 12). Ezekiel also rails against Edom for vengeance against Judah (Ezek 25:12 – 14), though this oracle is vague and difficult to date, and in any case makes nothing of Jacob and Esau's filial relationship. The oracle against Mount Seir in Ezek 35:1 – 15 was undoubtedly given after the fall of Jerusalem and obviously deals with the same issue as Obadiah, though again he makes nothing of the brotherly relationship. Juxtaposed with Ezek 36:1 – 16, here the focus is geographic; Mount Seir (metonymy for Edom) is juxtaposed with the mountains of Israel.

18. Compare also the opening of these oracles:

Jeremiah 49:7a-b	Obadiah 1b
Concerning Edom, Thus says YHWH Sebaoth	Thus says Adonay YHWH concerning Edom

speaks as a representative of a group, perhaps of the people as a whole, or of a cadre of faithful followers of YHWH in post-fall Jerusalem.

But what is the report? While the word שְׁמוּעָ itself does not help much,[19] the answer is given in v. 1d. The important detail to note is that like the oracle that Obadiah is about to declare, and like the message that the present messenger delivers, this report — that is, the report that a message had been sent to the nations — also came from YHWH. YHWH has let Obadiah and his colleagues in on a secret concerning Edom's fate, and on the way divine providence is exercised.

In v. 1d we learn some of the content of the report: an envoy has been sent among the nations. The word צִיר occurs only six times in the OT. Its meaning is suggested by Prov 13:17, where it is paired with "messenger" (מַלְאָךְ), and by all the other texts, where it is associated with the verb "to send" (שָׁלַח).[20] Obadiah does not explain who this messenger might be, but it is best to see here a reference to an angelic member of the heavenly council. Perhaps Obadiah saw a scene like that described in 1 Kgs 22:19 – 23, where Micaiah ben Imlah saw YHWH seated on his throne surrounded by his council. In that passage YHWH was seeking their counsel for a way to get Ahab to engage the Arameans in battle over Ramoth Gilead so that he might fall in battle. When one of those council members volunteered to be a deceptive spirit to entice him into going to war, YHWH sent him out.[21]

The envoy's message is summarized in v. 1e with one word in Hebrew, "Rise up!" (שָׁלַח). We might interpret this as a cryptic summary of Jeremiah's version of the divine summons to battle, "Gather together and come against her, and rise up for the battle." The notion of YHWH summoning the nations to battle on his behalf is common in the OT. We find fuller versions of such a summons in Jer 51:27 – 28 and Joel 4:9 – 11[3:9 – 11].

> Raise a standard in the land,
>> blow the trumpet among the nations;
> prepare the nations for war against her,
>> summon against her the kingdoms,
>> Ararat, Minni, and Ashkenaz;
> appoint a marshal against her,
>> bring up horses like bristling locusts.
> Prepare the nations for war against her,
>> the kings of the Medes, with their governors
>> and deputies,
>> and every land under their dominion.
>>   (Jer. 51:27 – 28, NRSV)

> Proclaim this among the nations:
> Prepare war,
>> stir up the warriors.
> Let all the soldiers draw near,
>> let them come up.
> Beat your plowshares into swords,
>> and your pruning hooks into spears;
>> let the weakling say, "I am a warrior."
> Come quickly,
>> all you nations all around,
>> gather yourselves there.
> Bring down your warriors, O YHWH.
>>   (Joel 4:9 – 11[3:9 – 11], NRSV)

Given the context in which Obadiah is ministering, the present statement is striking. Only recently his own people had been the victims of a host of armies whom YHWH had summoned to punish Judah for her rebellion against him and in

---

19. The word is relatively rare, and may be linked to good news (1 Sam 2:24; Prov 15:30; 25:25) or bad (Ps 112:7; Jer 49:23), to factual reports (1 Sam 4:19; 2 Sam 4:4; 13:30; 1 Kgs 2:28) or rumors (2 Kgs 19:7 = Isa 37:7; Ezek 7:26; 21:12[7]).

20. Isa 18:2; 57:9; Jer 49:14; Obad 1; Prov 25:13. The word is also cognate to Akkadian ṣiru, "envoy" (CAD 16.213).

21. On this text, see Block, "What Has Delphi to Do with Samaria?" 189 – 216.

fulfillment of the covenant curses declared centuries earlier by Moses in Deut 28:47 – 67. Now he is summoning them against Edom, which means that when Edom falls to Nabonidus (in 553 BC), this too will be an act of the sovereign God of Israel.

Although some interpret v. 1f as a continuation of the envoy's message for the nations, as in Jeremiah's parallel text,[22] the change in person suggests a change in speaker.[23] In fact, apart from the conjunction on the verb, what follows is exactly what we would expect of those who respond positively to the summons; they express their enthusiasm for the battle to which they are called.[24] Whereas in the rest of this book Obadiah treats Edom as masculine, "against her" (עָלֶיהָ) considers Edom to be feminine. Some who understand the book to reflect a liturgical cult drama see in the feminine suffix an allusion to Tiamat, the primeval foe whose defeat by Marduk was celebrated in Babylon at the annual New Years (Akitu) festival.[25]

However, the explanation is much simpler than that. It relates to the way OT writers refer to national entities. When they speak about the population, especially when they identify a nation by the name of its ancestor, they regularly perceive the nation as masculine. But since geographic entities are regularly considered feminine, when they use the feminine (as in this case), the territorial significance of the name appears to be primary.[26] And this should not surprise us. In the ANE, when nations planned campaigns of conquest, they generally thought of invading territory rather than attacking a people group.[27]

---

22. Raabe, *Obadiah*, 116; Barton, *Joel and Obadiah*, 134; Niehaus, "Obadiah," 512; Stuart, *Hosea-Jonah*, 410.

23. Otherwise the envoy volunteers with the nations. Wolff (*Obadiah and Jonah*, 47) suggests the plural first person cohortative refers to a majority of prophets in Jerusalem and their congregation.

24. Raabe (*Obadiah*, 116) suggests that after an imperative the *waw* conjunction + cohortative (וְנָקוּמָה) expresses purpose. However, "Rise, that we may rise against her for battle," makes no sense, and the conjunction must serve a different discourse function, perhaps equivalent to הִנֵּה, expressing a positive response. Renkema (*Obadiah*, 121) interprets the *waw* to imply "an explicit declaration or assurance."

25. M. Bic, "Zur Problematik des Buches Obadja" (VTSup 1; Leiden: Brill, 1953), 14.

26. Edom occurs with feminine verbs in Jer 49:17; Mal 1:4; with feminine pronominal suffixes that refer to Edom, see Ezek 25:13; 32:29; 35:15; Obad 1.

27. This renders all the more remarkable the ethnic rather than geographic determinative before "Israel" in the Merneptah Stela that lists the territories he conquered in the thirteenth century BC. See *COS* 2.41.

2

Obadiah 2 – 10

B. The Judgment:
Esau's Humiliation on His "Day" of Doom

Main Idea of the Passage

Though Esau prides himself in his independence and security, because of violence to his brother on his day of doom, YHWH will personally bring him down and cut him off forever. But YHWH will involve the nations who may be allied with Esau now. They will treacherously pillage all Esau's resources and drive him from his own land.

Literary Context

Having opened with the citation formula (v. 1b), YHWH's actual message is put on hold as the prophet offers some important background information. Based on the report Obadiah and his colleagues have received, we learn of YHWH's fundamentally hostile disposition toward Edom.

The actual "vision" announced in v. 1a is introduced in v. 2a with the focus particle, "See" (הִנֵּה). Thereafter the prophet envisions a horrific outburst of divine fury, climaxing in a summary statement of cause and effect (v. 10). Whereas v. 1f had suggested the target of YHWH's wrath was a specific land, now we learn it is actually a people whose identity is bound up with the personal name Esau. Verses 2 – 14 constitute a judgment speech against Esau. However, unlike most judgment speeches, which begin with the indictment and follow up with the sentence, here YHWH (who speaks in first person) reverses the order, declaring the sentence first (vv. 2 – 10) and then reviewing the evidence against Esau (vv. 11 – 14). He returns to the sentence briefly in vv. 15 – 18, and then concludes with a summary of the implications for Esau's demise for Israel and Judah (vv. 19 – 21).

Translation and Exegetical Outline

(See pages 58–59.)

Structure and Literary Form

This entire unit is held together by the treatment of Edom as an individual, Esau by name, and the motif of Esau's demise. Introduced by the focus particle ("See," v. 2a), the prophet achieves a powerful rhetorical effect by painting a series of word pictures that readers have no difficulty concretizing in their minds: (1) a secure settlement high up on the rocks (v. 3a-c); (2) vultures nesting high up (v. 4a-c); (3) burglars breaking into a house at night (v. 5a-d); (4) harvesters gathering grapes (v. 5e-f); (5) ransacked storerooms (v. 6); (6) friends driving people off their own territory (v. 7a-c); (7) people who once ate together trapping and being trapped (v. 7d); and (8) expressions of panic and shame (vv. 9a, 10b).

However, in terms of content, this section exhibits a clear a-b-a pattern, with descriptions of victimization at the hands of human enemies (vv. 5 – 7) sandwiched between descriptions of victimization at the hands of YHWH (vv. 2 – 4, 8 – 10). This division is reinforced by insertions of the signatory formula at the boundaries: at the very end of the first part (v. 4d) and near the beginning of the third part (v. 8b).[1] The boundary between the second and third parts is strengthened first by the insertion of "he has no clue!" at v. 7e, which refers strangely to Esau in the third person singular and shifts the focus from the treacherous allies to Edom's response, and second by the truncated interrogative construction of v. 8a, "Will [I] not on that day …?" but which is immediately cut off by the signatory formula. Obadiah's penchant for cutting off a thought by inserting an erratic[2] mid-sentence is also evident in v. 5c, "How you have been destroyed!" These all seem to reflect the excitement of the prophet in the original rhetorical situation or the excitement of the editor responsible for transcribing his prophecies.

---

1. Watts (*Obadiah*, 34 – 35, 49 – 50) mistakenly moves the formula to the end of v. 10, assuming it normally appears at the end of an oracle. See further below.

2. I use the term "erratic" in its geological sense. An erratic is a rock that has been picked up by a glacier and deposited in a new environment, where it differs in composition and shape from the rocks surrounding it.

Obadiah 2–10

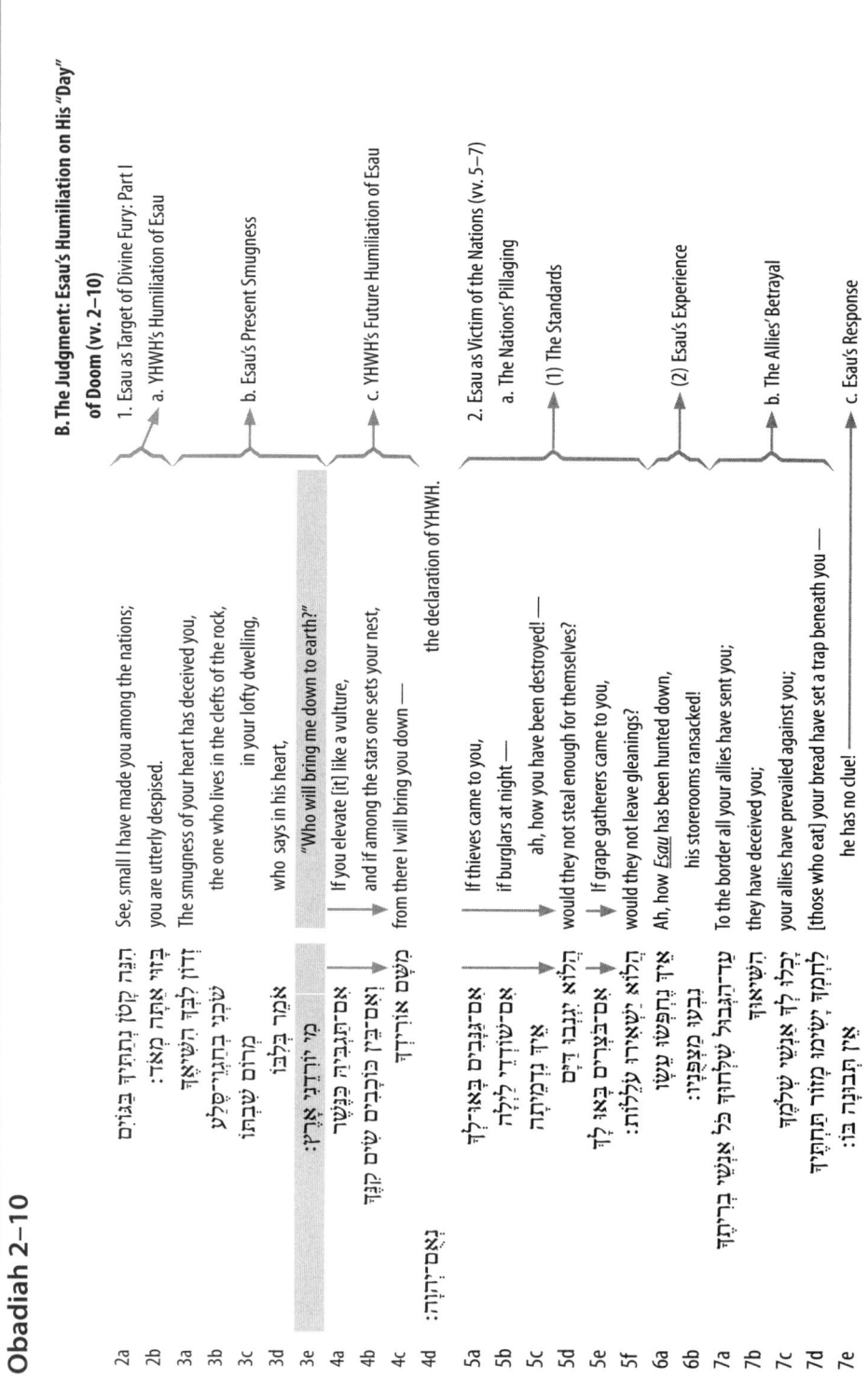

B. The Judgment: Esau's Humiliation on His "Day" of Doom (vv. 2–10)

1. Esau as Target of Divine Fury: Part I
   - a. YHWH's Humiliation of Esau
   - b. Esau's Present Smugness
   - c. YHWH's Future Humiliation of Esau

2. Esau as Victim of the Nations (vv. 5–7)
   - a. The Nations' Pillaging
     - (1) The Standards
     - (2) Esau's Experience
   - b. The Allies' Betrayal
   - c. Esau's Response

2a See, small I have made you among the nations;
2b you are utterly despised.
3a The smugness of your heart has deceived you,
3b the one who lives in the clefts of the rock,
3c in your lofty dwelling,
3d who says in his heart,
3e "Who will bring me down to earth?"
4a If you elevate [it] like a vulture,
4b and if among the stars one sets your nest,
4c from there I will bring you down —
4d the declaration of YHWH.
5a If thieves came to you,
5b if burglars at night —
5c ah, how you have been destroyed! —
5d would they not steal enough for themselves?
5e If grape gatherers came to you,
5f would they not leave gleanings?
6a Ah, how *Esau* has been hunted down,
6b his storerooms ransacked!
7a To the border all your allies have sent you;
7b they have deceived you;
7c your allies have prevailed against you;
7d [those who eat] your bread have set a trap beneath you —
7e he has no clue!

3. Esau as Target of Divine Fury II (vv. 8–10)

	Hebrew	Translation	Structure
8a	הֲלוֹא בַּיּוֹם הַהוּא	Will not on that day —	
8b	נְאֻם־יְהוָה	the declaration of YHWH,	
8c	וְהַאֲבַדְתִּי חֲכָמִים מֵאֱדוֹם	— I destroy the wise from Edom,	a. The Nature of YHWH's Action against Esau
8d	וּתְבוּנָה מֵהַר עֵשָׂו׃	and understanding from Mount _Esau?_	
9a	וְחַתּוּ גִבּוֹרֶיךָ תֵּימָן	Then your heroes will panic, O Teman,	
9b	לְמַעַן יִכָּרֶת־אִישׁ מֵהַר עֵשָׂו מִקָּטֶל׃	so every man will be cut off from Mount _Esau._	b. The Effect of YHWH's Action against Esau
10a	מֵחֲמַס אָחִיךָ יַעֲקֹב	Because of murder,	
10b		violence against your _brother_ Jacob,	
10c	תְּכַסְּךָ בוּשָׁה	shame shall cover you,	
10d	וְנִכְרַתָּ לְעוֹלָם׃	and you shall be cut off forever.	c. The Reason for YHWH's Action against Esau

Explanation of the Text

1. Esau as Target of Divine Fury: Part I (vv. 2 – 4)

This oracle proper opens with the focus particle, "See" (traditionally "Behold"; הִנֵּה), which often introduces surprising events or significant changes of perspective.[3] This strong opening may have been necessitated by the cynicism and disillusionment of Obadiah's immediate audience of Judahites, who have survived the disasters of 586 BC but are angry with YHWH for having abandoned them in their hour of greatest need. What follows is a systematic portrayal of YHWH's response to Esau, who had not only stood by while it happened, but had also actively participated in Jerusalem's fall.

Building on the messenger's call in v. 1e, this is a remarkable text, in which we hear YHWH threaten Judah's enemy with humiliation and annihilation. However, we do not learn why he is the target of the divine fury until v. 10a: "because of murder, violence against your brother Jacob." But this statement is so general it simply raises more questions: What sort of violence? In what context? With what consequences? The answers are delayed until the following section.

Obadiah's dependence on Jeremiah continues, though this time he draws on a different section of his predecessor's oracle concerning Edom.

If anything, Obadiah's reading is smoother than Jeremiah's,[4] as well as fuller and more dramatic. The addition of the internal speech, "Who will bring me down to earth?" (v. 3e), sets the stage for YHWH's

action at the end, and the addition of "among the stars one sets your nest" heightens the contrast between Esau's present state and his destiny.

Like the subunit in which this section is embedded (vv. 2 – 10), this paragraph exhibits an a-b-a pattern; the image of Esau's arrogance (v. 3) is sandwiched between two images of YHWH's determination to bring Esau down (vv. 2, 4). The paragraph is carefully constructed so that v. 2 declares the theme, v. 3 describes the present problem, and v. 4 announces YHWH's answer to the Esau's challenge in v. 3e. As a whole vv. 2 – 4 presents brilliant commentary on the first half of Ezekiel's gnomic declaration in Ezek 17:24: "I bring low the high tree; I make high the low tree."[5]

a. YHWH's humiliation of Esau (v. 2). The grammatical construction of the opening clause highlights the effect of YHWH's actions by fronting the predicate.[6] When YHWH is through with Esau objectively, he will be insignificant among the nations, and "utterly despised." The first term ("small," קָטֹן) places Esau in the same category as Israel/Jacob, which Amos characterizes as defenseless against YHWH's judgment (Amos 7:2, 5). If Obadiah had used the feminine suffix or was referring to Edom rather than Esau, this could point to a reduction in territory — a response to their encroachment on Judah's territory as their end was approaching (Ezek 35:10 – 15; 36:2) — or the devastation of the landscape (Ezek 35:3 – 9, 15). Because

---

3. Cf. C. H. J. van der Merwe, J. A. Naudé, and J. H. Kroeze, *A Biblical Hebrew Reference Grammar* (Biblical Languages: Hebrew 3; Sheffield: Sheffield Academic, 2004), 330.

4. He softens the opening by removing the *kî* particle (I interpret *kî* in Jeremiah asseveratively; cf. Jack R. Lundbom, *Jeremiah 37 – 52: A New Translation with Introduction and Commentary* [AB 21C; New York: Doubleday, 2004], 338), drops the awkward "the terror you inspire," and replaces "who

claims the top of a hill" with "in your lofty dwelling," a parallel phrase for "in the clefts of a rock."

5. Cf. 1 Sam 2:7; 2 Sam 22:28 = Ps 18:28[27]; Pss 75:8[7]; 147:6; Isa 2:11, 12, 17; 26:5; also Sir 7:11.

6. As opposed to constructions like הִנֵּה אֲנִי נְתַתִּי קָטֹן בַּגּוֹיִם, "See, I am making you small among the nations," which highlight the subject.

Jeremiah 49:15 – 16	Obadiah 2 – 4
Indeed see, small I have made you among the nations, despised among humankind.	See, small I have made you among the nations; You are utterly despised.
The terror you inspire has deceived you — the smugness of your heart — the one who lives in the clefts of *the* rock, who claims the top of the hill. *Though* you make *your nest* high like the vulture,	The smugness of your heart *has deceived you*, the one who lives in the clefts of *a* rock, in your lofty dwelling, *the one who says in his heart,* *"Who will bring me down to earth?"* **If** you elevate [it] like the vulture, *and if among the stars one sets your nest,*
from there I will bring you down — the declaration of YHWH.	from there I will bring you down — the declaration of YHWH.

כִּי־הִנֵּה קָטֹן נְתַתִּיךָ בַּגּוֹיִם
בָּזוּי בָּאָדָם
תִּפְלַצְתְּךָ הִשִּׁיא אֹתָךְ
זְדוֹן לִבֶּךָ
שֹׁכְנִי בְחַגְוֵי הַסֶּלַע
תֹּפְשִׂי מְרוֹם גִּבְעָה

כִּי־תַגְבִּיהַּ כַּנֶּשֶׁר קִנֶּךָ

מִשָּׁם אוֹרִידְךָ
נְאֻם־יְהֹוָה

הִנֵּה קָטֹן נְתַתִּיךָ בַּגּוֹיִם
בָּזוּי אַתָּה מְאֹד

זְדוֹן לִבְּךָ הִשִּׁיאֶךָ
שֹׁכְנִי בְחַגְוֵי־סֶלַע
מְרוֹם שִׁבְתּוֹ
אֹמֵר בְּלִבּוֹ
מִי יוֹרִדֵנִי אָרֶץ
אִם־תַּגְבִּיהַ כַּנֶּשֶׁר
וְאִם־בֵּין כּוֹכָבִים שִׂים קִנֶּךָ
מִשָּׁם אוֹרִידְךָ
נְאֻם־יְהֹוָה

he is speaking to Esau, who smugly boasts of his independence and security (v. 3) and in the end will be cut off from Mount Esau (vv. 9b, 10d), the statement could refer to the decimation of Edom's population.[7] However, since Hebrew uses a different expression for reduction of population,[8] this should be interpreted as a sociological statement, referring to Esau's status "among the nations." Most commentators interpret the perfect verb ("have made"; נְתַתִּיךָ) as a prophetic perfect, referring to

YHWH's future action that is so certain Obadiah can speak of it as if it were already accomplished.[9] However, since YHWH has already summoned the nations against Esau (v. 1e), certainly in his mind Esau's diminished status is a current reality.[10] Verse 2b declares that this is true also of the nations, who presently hold Esau in utter contempt. Obadiah modifies the parallelism in Jeremiah's statement ("Despised [I have made] you among humankind") to highlight how despicable Esau is to the nations.

---

7. The statement may also allude to Gen 27:1, 15, which refer to Esau as Isaac and Rebekah's greater, i.e., older (הַגָּדֹל) son, in contrast to Jacob who is smaller/younger (הַקָּטָן) son.

8. הִמְעִיט, Lev 26:22; Ps 107:38; Jer 10:24; Ezek 29:15.

9. On the prophetic perfect, see Max Rogland, *Alleged Non-Past Uses of* Qatal *in Classical Hebrew* (Studia Semitica Neerlandica; Assen: Royal Van Gorcum, 2003), 53 – 114.

10. So also ibid., 106; Raabe, *Obadiah*, 121.

The verbless clause construction reinforces the sense of present status.

b. Esau's present smugness (v. 3). YHWH could have moved directly to v. 4 for clarification on what he means by making Esau small and despised. Instead, he inserts an observation on Esau's own present disposition, which he characterizes as overweening but delusional self-confidence. He begins with a thesis statement (v. 3a), and then offers two expressions of this smugness (v. 3b-c and 3d-e).

On first sight v. 3a might suggest that Esau's pride drove YHWH to seek his destruction. Indeed, elsewhere pride is deemed a damnable offence.[11] However, in view of v. 10a and the exposition of this statement in vv. 11 – 14, Esau's primary crime is not his arrogance. This verse describes Esau's sense of imperviousness to any outsider affecting his well-being or status. His disposition is characterized as "smugness of heart." As elsewhere, the word לֵב should not be limited to "heart," that is, the seat of emotions or will, but it includes the seat of thought as well — hence the later reference to speaking "in [one's] heart" (v. 3d). Hebrew לֵב represents one's inner being, from which arise dispositions, attitudes, thoughts, actions, and speech.[12] The smug attitude itself is expressed with זָדוֹן, which elsewhere refers to presumptuousness and insolent self-confidence.[13]

Here Obadiah has simplified Jeremiah's counterpart (Jer 49:16), dropping the hapax תִּפְלַצְתְּךָ, "your terror" (i.e., "the terror you create") and making "smugness" the subject of the verb "to deceive." In YHWH's mind, whatever terror Esau might create in others has now become irrelevant. Nevertheless, Esau's smugness is neither coincidental nor impulsive; he has let himself be led astray by it. The meaning of the hiphil form of נָשָׁא (הִשִּׁיא), "to deceive, delude, give false hope," is illustrated dramatically by Eve's comment concerning the serpent, "The serpent deceived me, and I ate" (Gen 3:13). This kind of false hope involves believing a lie and trusting in people or things that fail to deliver what they promise.[14]

The remainder of v. 3 involves two subordinate clauses that clarify Esau's pompous self-confidence. Although they exhibit a somewhat parallel construction (both begin with participles in apposition to v. 3a), they serve different functions. The first adds a vivid image of Esau's secure home high up on the rocks of Edom, supposedly out of reach of any who have ideas of invasion. Following the lead of Jeremiah, Obadiah strengthens the rhetorical force of his statement with vivid local coloring. His reference to Esau's home as "your lofty dwelling" and in "the clefts of the rock" reflects an awareness of the topography of the region. Although the territory of Edom includes level terrain, some of the major settlements, including the later Nabatean capital at Petra, were built on elevated rock outcrops with steep slopes. Whether סֶלַע functions as a generic expression for inaccessible rocky terrain or as a proper noun Sela, which stands for the capital, the description would have made sense to Obadiah's audience. Which came first, Esau's smugness because of his invulnerable dwelling, or his invulnerable dwelling as an expression of his smugness, is not clear.

---

11. Isa 2:11 – 17; 16:6 – 14; Ezek 28:2 – 10; 28:12 – 19; Amos 6:8; Mal 3:19[4:1].

12. Cf. the Shema, where לֵב is juxtaposed with נֶפֶשׁ ("being, person") and מְאֹד ("resources"). In Jesus' citation of the Shema in Mark 12:29 – 30 he renders Hebrew לֵב with two Greek words: καρδία ("heart") and διάνοια ("mind").

13. Deut 17:12; 18:22; 1 Sam 17:28; Prov 11:2; 21:24; Ezek 7:10; Sir 7:6.

14. Cf. Sennacherib's taunt of Hezekiah's envoys: "Don't let the god you depend on deceive you when he says, 'Jerusalem will not be given into the hands of the king of Assyria'" (2 Kgs 19:10; cf. also 18:29).

According to v. 3d-e, Esau's disposition is un-ambiguous. Incorporating a feature typical of He-brew narrative, Obadiah strengthens the rhetorical force of Jeremiah's utterance by portraying Esau as a character in the plot whose attitudes are reflected in direct speech. From his speech we may draw our conclusions regarding his state of mind. However, in this instance Esau has no conversation partner; this is internal speech located in the seat of his problem, his heart/mind. Indeed the idiom "to say in/to one's heart" often simply concretizes the no-tion of thought.

Esau asks himself a rhetorical question: "Who will bring me down to earth?" Questions like this are not asked to solicit information or to encour-age discussion; rather, they actually express a strong conviction. Anticipating a negative answer, in effect Esau says, "No one can bring me down to earth." The word אֶרֶץ bears a wide range of mean-ings: earth, land (in contrast to sea), territory, ground, and even the netherworld.[15] This seems to be either a hyperbolic expression according to which Esau perceives himself living high in the heavens (cf. v. 4b), in contrast to earth, or he lives on a high and inaccessible mountain, in contrast to the ground/territory where ordinary mortals live.

c. YHWH's future humiliation of Esau (v. 4). In either case, Esau has here issued a challenge that YHWH cannot resist. Picking up on the topo-graphical imagery, he ups the ante with two hy-pothetical clauses arranged in modified elliptical though climactic parallelism. While most transla-tions understand the first line (v. 4a) to concern

an eagle[16] soaring in the sky, the hiphil causative verb תַּגְבִּיהַ, "to raise, elevate," requires an object, namely, to elevate something, leaving the hearer to fill in the gap. Obadiah can do this because he as-sumes his hearers are familiar with Jer 49:16: "If you make your nest high like the vulture." Apart from beginning with a different particle ("if" [אִם] rather than "though"[כִּי]), in the consonantal text Obadiah's and Jeremiah's wording is identical. The notion of vultures' nests secure in the heights of the mountains is well established in the OT and is illustrated graphically in Job 39:27 – 28:

> Is it at your command that the eagle mounts up
>   and makes its nest on high?
> It lives on the rock
>   and makes its home in the fastness of the
>   rocky crag. (NRSV)

The second line (v. 4b) dispels any doubts about Obadiah's intention, for now we see what he has done with Jeremiah's statement. To reassure and encourage his hearers he drops the object down to the second line and constructs a new clause inten-sifying the imagery: "and if among the stars one sets your nest" (וְאִם בֵּין כּוֹכָבִים שִׂים קִנֶּךָ). If the first line offers a reasonable picture of vultures' building nests high up in the peaks of the rock mentioned in v. 3b or in trees at the top of the rock, then the second line is hyperbolic, extending the potential home for the birds up in the sky among the stars.[17] The prophet's reference to extreme heights among the stars speaks of Esau's claim to absolute inac-cessibility, invulnerability, and invincibility. No one can touch him!

---

15. Isa 26:19; 44:23; Jonah 2:7[6]; Ps 22:30[29]; Job 17:16. Cf. variations of expressions like "the netherworld" (תַּחְתִּיּוֹת אֶרֶץ): Ps 139:15; 63:10[9]; Ezek 26:20; 32:18, 24.

16. The word נֶשֶׁר seems to have functioned as a generic expression for large birds of prey, including several different species of eagles (Deut 32:11; Isa 40:31; Ezek 17:3, 4), as well as scavenging vultures, like the griffon vulture (Mic 1:16). Both types of birds are known for soaring high in the sky. In any

case, when soaring high in the sky they may not be distinguish-able to the untrained eye. The vulture, which nests in rocky crags, is intended here (see *Encyclopaedia Judaica*, 20:589).

17. We may interpret the verb שִׂים either as an infinitive absolute functioning as a verb with the subject assumed from the previous line (Raabe, *Obadiah*, 133), or a passive participle, as in Num 24:21 (Renkema, *Obadiah*, 131).

Oh yeah? With brutal efficiency (a mere two words in Hebrew) YHWH declares his resolve, not to punish Esau for his arrogance (see v. 10a), but to challenge his smug sense of invulnerability. Accepting the challenge of Esau's rhetorical question in v. 3e, the declaration is emphatic: "from there" (מִשָּׁם) YHWH will bring Esau down. YHWH's response is reminiscent of his comment concerning Israel in Amos 9:2:

> Though they dig into Sheol,
> from there shall my hand take them;
> though they climb up to heaven,
> from there I will bring them down. (NRSV).

Once YHWH has set his sights on a target, there is no escape.

Obadiah closes this segment of his oracle with the signatory formula, "the declaration of YHWH" (נְאֻם יהוה). Variations of this formula occur 365 times in the OT, with Jeremiah (175x) accounting for almost one-half and Ezekiel (85x) one-fourth of these.[18] In twenty instances the formula appears at the end of an oracle that has been introduced by the citation formula. The rhetorical equivalence of citation and signatory formulae is suggested by Ezek 13:6–7 and 22:28, which portray false prophets using both to authenticate their messages. As in our text, on twenty-seven occasions in Ezekiel the phrase functions as an end-of-paragraph marker, alerting the reader to a change of topic within an oracle. In the remaining occurrences it appears mid-verse, interrupting the flow of pronouncements for heightened rhetorical effect.[19]

While the etymology of נְאֻם remains uncertain, its rhetorical function is clear.[20] Whether attached at the end of an oracle or inserted within divine speech, this formula adds solemnity to the prophetic pronouncement by pointing to its divine source. Indeed it seems to function as a verbal signature, placing the divine imprimatur on the oral word, analogous to the inscribed signature or seal imprint of an authority behind a written text. Obadiah's vision of Edom's demise does not arise from his own imagination. It comes from YHWH, and the prophet declares it with divine authorization.

2. Esau as Victim of the Nations (vv. 5–7)

Having heard YHWH's announcement that he will bring Esau down, we expect to see him act. Instead in these verses he is out of the picture entirely — unless of course we interpret "How you have been destroyed!" as a divine passive. This segment portrays Esau exclusively as the victim of other nations' actions against him.

Obadiah's portrayal of the nations begins with a statement on how thieves and pillagers normally operate (v. 5a-b, d-f), and then contrasts this with how outsiders have treated Esau (vv. 6a–7d). He interrupts the description with an exclamatory interjection (v. 5c), and concludes with a terse statement of Esau's response (v. 7e).

a. The nations' pillaging (vv. 5–6). Obadiah's portrait of the nations' attack on Esau consists of two parts: a statement involving thieves and harvesters describing how people typically lay hold on property (v. 5), followed by a statement on how the nations have laid hold of Esau's property (v. 6). In the first we recognize again the influence of Jeremiah's earlier utterances (see table on p. 65).

Again Obadiah is not slavishly bound to Jeremiah's wording, but modifies his statements to suit

---

18. For discussion of the frequency, distribution, and significance of the formula see D. Vetter, "neʾūm Ausspruch," *THAT* 2:1–3; F. Baumgärtel, "Die Formel neʾum Jahwe," *ZAW* 73 (1961): 277–90.

19. See, e.g., Jer 34:17.

20. The vocalization and consistent appearance of נְאֻם in construct with another noun, usually the divine name, point to a substantive significance for the term, rather than the common verbal rendering, "declares the Lord Yahweh." The verb (denominative) appears only in Jer 23:31.

Jeremiah 49:9	Obadiah 5
If grape-gatherers came to you, would they not leave gleanings?	If thieves came to you, if burglars at night — ah, how you have been destroyed! — would they not steal enough for themselves?
If thieves came by night, would they not destroy enough for themselves?	If grape gatherers came to you, would they not leave gleanings?
אִם־בֹּצְרִים בָּאוּ לָךְ לֹא יַשְׁאִרוּ עוֹלֵלוֹת	אִם־גַּנָּבִים בָּאוּ־לְךָ אִם־שׁוֹדְדֵי לַיְלָה אֵיךְ נִדְמֵיתָה הֲלוֹא יִגְנְבוּ דַיָּם אִם־בֹּצְרִים בָּאוּ לָךְ הֲלוֹא יַשְׁאִירוּ עֹלֵלוֹת
אִם־גַּנָּבִים בַּלַּיְלָה הִשְׁחִיתוּ דַיָּם	

the new context[21] and to intensify their rhetorical force: adding a parallel line to v. 5a, inserting an emotional interjection (v. 5c), smoothing Jeremiah's awkward reference to destroying (הִשְׁחִיתוּ) enough for themselves to stealing (גָּנַב) enough for themselves, and transposing the images of thieves and grape harvesters.

Obadiah's two examples of how people acquire goods involve illegitimate seizure and apparently negotiated acquisition. At this point he is not talking about Esau's losses to enemy armies, but to common every day/night occurrences, though his expression שׁוֹדְדֵי לַיְלָה (lit., "destroyers of the night") certainly prepares the way for v. 6a. The word שָׁדַד means "to take by force, destroy" and is often used of invading armies (Jer 49:28; Ezek 32:12), or of YHWH destroying the enemy (Jer 25:36; 47:4; 51:55). However, since Obadiah envisions clandestine attacks, he must intend this expression as a virtual synonym for "thieves" (גַּנָּבִים). His addi-

tion of this line intensifies Jeremiah's statement and sets the stage for the principal clause (v. 5d), which highlights how ordinary thieves typically operate. When they are satisfied with the property[22] they have stolen, they stop. They take only that which they consider valuable for their purposes and then hurry away, leaving the rest behind.

The same principle applies to harvesters in the vineyard. They tend to concentrate on healthy clusters of grapes and leave behind on the vines the small and individual grapes and on the ground those that have fallen either before or in the process of picking. They do not take everything, but leave the latter for gleaners (עֹלֵלוֹת). Indeed within Israel's constitution Israelite landowners were prohibited from returning to the field to pick the remnants and required to leave them for the economically marginalized.[23] But "grape gatherers" not only leave the remnants of the fruit; they also leave the vines standing. They do not destroy everything

---

21. Feminine לָךְ in Jeremiah (referring to the land of Edom) becomes masculine לְךָ in Obad 5a. However, in v. 5e, where the citation is more precise, Obadiah retains Jeremiah's feminine, perhaps because the Hebrew word for vineyard (כֶּרֶם) may be considered feminine (Lev 25:3; Isa 27:2). Thus Renkema, *Obadiah*, 137.

22. Hebrew דַיָּם, lit., "their sufficiency," that is, as much as they want or need. Cf. Exod 36:5, 7.

23. Lev 19:9 – 10; 23:22; Deut 24:19 – 21; cf. Ruth 2:2 – 23.

in sight. In fact, owners of vineyards generally hire the harvesters; the latter are not plunderers or thieves. Under normal circumstances the relationship between the two parties would be friendly, if not contractual. If the image of thieves contrasts with that of v. 6, the image of grape harvesters contrasts with the allies' treachery in v. 7a-d.

However, in the meantime Obadiah is so keyed up over the image of Esau's devastation that before he finishes his first image, he interrupts his own train of thought with an excited interjection: "Ah, how you have been destroyed!"[24] The particle אֵיךְ, which reflects the prophet's disposition toward Esau's demise, is often used to express mourning,[25] or shock and horror.[26] Although it involves the ruin of Jerusalem rather than Esau, Jer 9:19 offers a remarkably parallel context:

> For a sound of wailing is heard from Zion:
> "How we are [plundered] [שֻׁדָּדְנוּ]!
> We are utterly shamed,
> because we have left the land,
> because they have cast down our dwellings.
> (NRSV)

Many interpret this clause as an exclamation of *Schadenfreude*, joy over another person's grief.[27] However, not only is the word אֵיךְ never employed this way, but also when joy is expressed over others' grief, it is explicitly declared in the text.[28] But why would YHWH and Obadiah express horror rather than glee over the demise of Esau? After all, as we will see, as he has done to others, so it is done to

him (v. 15a-b). Perhaps it reflects a higher ethic, like that expressed by Job in Job 31:29 – 30:

> If I have rejoiced at the ruin of those who hated me,
>   or exulted when evil overtook them —
> I have not let my mouth sin
>   by asking for their lives with a curse. (NRSV)

Perhaps both YHWH and Obadiah rue the calamity of Jacob's brother; after all, he too is a son of Isaac and a grandson of Abraham.

In v. 6 we discover why the prophet is dismayed: Esau has been pillaged and ransacked. The switch to the third person reflects the prophet's rhetorical situation. On the one hand, he declares YHWH's message to Esau as his hypothetical audience. On the other hand, outbursts like this remind us that his primary audience is his own people, either the pathetic remnant in Jerusalem or his country folk scattered abroad, in whom the hope for Israel's future rests. He expresses shock at what has happened to Esau; he has been hunted down.[29] Amos 9:3 offers a vivid illustration of the word as used in this context:

> Though they hide themselves on the top of
>   Carmel,
>   from there I will search out and take them;
> and though they hide from my sight at the
>   bottom of the sea,
>   there I will command the sea-serpent, and
>   it shall bite them. (NRSV)

The language is appropriate for people who are living in the caves and clefts of rocks, but who now

---

24. Hebrew נִדְמֵיתָה probably derives from a root דמה, "to destroy," and is often applied to ruined peoples or cities: Isa 6:5; 15:1; Jer 47:5; Hos 4:6; 10:7. However, some also suggest a link with the homonym דמה, "to be silent," in which case the exclamation is deliberately ambiguous, meaning either or both: (1) "How you are ruined!" (2) "How you are silenced!" Raabe, *Obadiah*, 142; Ben Zvi, *Obadiah*, 79 – 80. Some commentators smooth the reading by moving this interjection to the end of the verse since they break the flow of thought and anticipate the tone of v. 6 (Watts, *Obadiah*, 34), but this destroys the

rhetorical force of the interjection and imposes on the text a modern Western commitment to a certain definition of order.
25. 2 Sam 1:19, 25, 27; Isa 14:4, 12; Ezek 26:17.
26. Ps 73:19; Prov 5:12.
27. E.g., Raabe, *Obadiah*.
28. Lam 2:16 – 17; 4:21; Ezek 25:3, 6, 15; 35:15. So also Renkema, *Obadiah*, 137.
29. The verb חָפַשׂ denotes "to search, track down, hunt for diligently" (see Gen 31:35; 44:12; 1 Sam 23:23; 1 Kgs 20:6; 2 Kgs 10:23; Ps 77:7[6]; Zeph.1:12.

in the face of the invaders hide in the farthest crevasses and crannies.

So much for Esau himself, who represents the population. Continuing the family picture, Obadiah's gaze turns to Esau's domestic compound (v. 6b), which he discovers to be totally ransacked. To paint the picture he employs a hapax noun (a word that occurs nowhere else), מַצְפֻּן, which derives from a root צָפַן, "to hide, store," and cognate to the form צָפוּן, "treasured possession" (Ezek 7:22). The form of the present word with a *mem* prefix suggests a "place where treasured possessions are stored or hidden,"[30] perhaps an alternative to עוֹצָר, "storehouse."[31]

This statement also involves a rare verb, בָּעָה, "to enquire, search out," which occurs elsewhere only once (Isa 21:12). The verbal picture suggests enemies who have hunted down Esau in every hiding place in the land, scoured his home for treasures, and ransacked the place. Although Obadiah uses different words, this is his version of Jer 49:10, "But I am the one who stripped Esau bare, I have uncovered his hiding-places, *and should he [try to] hide, he will not succeed*. His offspring are destroyed, his kinsfolk and his neighbors; and he is no more" (italics added). Remarkably, where Jeremiah keeps the focus on YHWH as the one pursuing and destroying Esau, Obadiah highlights the role of the nations.

b. The allies' betrayal (v. 7a-d). This is confirmed in v. 7a-d. While this verse is extremely difficult to interpret,[32] the language seems heavily influenced by Jeremiah, whose words seem to be ringing in Obadiah's ears. This verse appears to offer commentary on the clause וְנֶחְבָּה לֹא יוּכָל, "and should he [try to] hide, he will not succeed." On first hearing this sounds like an elaboration on v. 6a, which paints an image of the enemies hunting down Edomites, presumably in their caves and crevasses. However, on further reflection, it seems that in the face of the invasion many Edomites had fled for refuge to their neighbors with whom they were allied.[33] But instead of finding protection, they were rebuffed by their own friends and sent back home to face their foes. It may be helpful to analyze this verse by asking two questions: (1) Who are these "allies"? (2) How did they respond to Esau when he was in distress?

Obadiah uses three expressions to identify the actors in this drama. First, they are (lit.) "all the men of your covenant" (כֹּל אַנְשֵׁי בְרִיתֶךָ; v. 7a). Although the first part, "all the men of," is common,[34] the nearest analogue to this expression occurs in Mal 2:14, where a wife is referred to as a "woman of your covenant" (אֵשֶׁת בְּרִיתֶךָ). The word בְּרִית refers to an agreement or pact between two parties. These parties may be equal, as in the case of the pact between Jacob and Laban in Gen. 31:44 (bilateral parity treaty), or unequal, as in the case of Nebuchadnezzar and Zedekiah in Ezek 17:13 – 19 (unilateral suzerainty treaty). Presumably the covenant alluded to here was of the former type (cf. Jer. 27:3).

---

30. LXX renders the expression *ta kekrummena* ("the hidden things"). Similarly Latin Vulgate, *abscondita eius*.

31. Note the references to the "treasures of the king" in 1 Kgs 14:26; also YHWH's storehouses in Deut 28:12; 32:34.

32. Many interpret v. 7a to mean that Edom's allies have joined the enemies in trying to drive the Edomites from their own land (Raabe, *Obadiah*, 149 – 50). Based on the verb שִׁלְּחוּךָ, "they sent you," Niehaus ("Obadiah," 521) argues this refers to the rejection of envoys who were sent to the allies to plead for support.

33. So also Renkema, *Joel and Obadiah*, 141 – 44; Barton, *Obadiah*, 140; Wolff, *Obadiah and Jonah*, 50 – 51.

34. See "all the men of war," i.e., "warriors," in Deut 2:16; Josh 5:4; 6:3; Joel 4:9[3:9]; "all the men of valor" (2 Kgs 24:16; Ps 76:6[5]; as well as "all the men of GN," that is, a geographic location. Gen 29:22; Deut 21:21; Josh 8:25; Judg 12:4; 1 Sam 11:1; or a people group, Ezra 10:9. Judges 9:49 refers to "all the men of the tower of Shechem," and Job 37:7 to "all the men he has made."

Second, they are "men of your peace" (אַנְשֵׁי שְׁלֹמֶךָ, v. 7c). In this association of "peace" and "covenant" Obadiah has separated two words that occur together elsewhere in the phrase "covenant of peace" (בְּרִית שָׁלוֹם).[35] This phrase suggests a formal agreement not only to settle hurtful scores, but a pact by which the parties declared their solidarity, friendship, and commitment to seek one another's well-being.[36]

Third, they are men "who eat your bread." The expression לַחְמְךָ, "your bread," is difficult and has led to all sorts of interpretations and conjectural changes to the text. Because the expression functions as a correlative of "all the men of your covenant" and "men of your peace," the word אַנְשֵׁי, "men of," may have dropped out accidentally. The same could be said for reconstructions like כְלֵי לַחְמְךָ, "those who eat your bread,"[37] or לֹחֲמֵי לַחְמְךָ, also "those who eat your bread."[38] However, the elliptical expression of MT may be intentional, assuming hearers will add "men of" in their minds, but heightening the rhetorical effect by sequenced shortening of the expressions, "all the men of your covenant" (three words); "the men of your peace" (two words); "your bread" (one word). "Your bread" may refer simply to expressions of hospitality and friendship by eating together,[39] but it seems more likely in context that this is shorthand for the entire covenant-making procedure, which typically climaxed in a meal celebrating the

relationship.[40] All three expressions refer to Esau's allies.

The response of the allies is also described with four expressions. First, they sent Esau back to his territory (v. 7a). We might have expected Obadiah to use the verb הֵשִׁיב, "to send back," except that the prepositional phrase "to the border" (עַד־הַגְּבוּל) suggests not a particular destination but simply out of their own territory, so these allies would not need to deal with the people of Esau. Furthermore, שִׁלַּח communicates more forcefully the sense of "dispatch."

Second, the allies have "deceived" Esau. The verb הִשִּׁיא (נָשָׁא in hiphil) means "to deceive" by giving false hopes. Presumably Esau's formalized "peace" with his allies involved not only a nonaggression agreement, but also a promise by the partners to defend each other in the face of external threats. For Esau this proved a false hope.

Third, they "have prevailed against" Esau. Here יָכֹל suggests forcefully imposing one's will on another person, thereby violating the letter and the spirit of the treaty. In this case it involved expelling them from the land rather than hosting them as friends.

Fourth, the allies "have set a trap" under Esau. This reading of מָזוֹר is admittedly tentative. Following the early versions,[41] it assumes a derivation from a root מזר, "to weave, twist."[42] Accordingly, not only have the allies sent Esau back to their land

---

35. Num 25:12; Isa 54:10; Ezek 34:25.

36. Cf. Ps 41:10[9], which speaks of "a man of my peace," as one in whom I trust.

37. A. B. Ehrlich, *Randglossen zur Hebräischen Bibel*, 5 (Leipzig: 1912), 259.

38. Hence a haplographic error (reading a word or letter once when it appears twice in the text before the translator). *BHS* suggests simply repointing the word, לֹחֲמֶיךָ. Cf. G. I. Davies, "A New Solution to a Crux in Obadiah 7," *VT* 27 (1977): 484 – 87. For further discussion, see A. Gelston, *The Twelve Minor Prophets* (BHQ 13; Stuttgart: Deutsche Bibelgesellschaft, 2010), 89*.

39. Gen 18:1 – 8; 24:33, 54; Ps 41:10[9] pairs "the one of my peace" with "the one who eats my bread."

40. E.g., Jacob and Laban, in Gen 31:54; cf. 2 Sam 3:12 – 21. Note especially the meal the Israelites ate in the presence of YHWH at Sinai, Exod 24:11.

41. LXX reads ἔνεδρα; Vulgate, *insidias*; Targum, תקלא; all of which mean "snare, trap, or ambush." Thus Wolff, *Obadiah and Jonah*, 35; Allen, *Joel, Obadiah, Jonah and Micah*, 150.

42. Allen, *Joel, Obadiah, Jonah and Micah*, 150. In Hebrew מָזוֹר means "wound, sore, ulcer" (Jer 30:13; Hos 5:13), but this makes no sense in context.

(to be caught by the invaders), but for those who have found refuge in their land, they have set traps as if they were wild animals.

c. Esau's response (v. 7e). This paragraph concludes with another surprising interjection, declaring Esau's response: אֵין תְּבוּנָה בּוֹ (lit., "There is no understanding in him"). Again the shift to the third person reflects the context: Obadiah's hypothetical audience may be Esau, but Obadiah is actually talking about him — rather than to him — to Obadiah's own country folk, either the remnant in Jerusalem with him or the scattered exiles. The statement is probably intentionally ambiguous. It could mean either that Esau has no clue about what is happening to and around him, or that he is dumbfounded by his allies' treachery, or both.

3. Esau as Target of Divine Fury: Part II (vv. 8 – 10)

Having described how the nations — both enemy and ally — contribute to Esau's downfall, in these verses the prophet's focus returns to the divine role. Continuing the triadic pattern we have observed earlier, this section subdivides into three parts, dealing respectively with the nature of YHWH's action against Esau (v. 8), the effect of YHWH's action against Esau (v. 9), and the reason for YHWH's action against Esau (v. 10).

a. The nature of YHWH's action against Esau (v. 8). The new segment opens awkwardly with הֲלוֹא בַּיּוֹם הַהוּא, lit., "Is it not on that day …?" Grammatically this is a question, but when rhetorical interrogatives begin with הֲלוֹא they often express certainty, and the phrase may actually be rendered positively, "Surely on that day. …"[43] This is the

first reference to "the day" in Obadiah. Whereas in vv. 11 – 14 the expression refers to "Jacob's day," that is, "the day of his doom/distress," and in v. 15a it refers to YHWH's day, that is, the day of his intervention, here Obadiah has in mind Esau's day, that is, the moment of his demise.

But once again, Obadiah immediately interrupts his train of thought with an interjection, this time the signatory formula (as in v. 4d). The insertion is awkward, and many have moved the formula to a more natural location, perhaps at the end of v. 10.[44] However, placed here the phrase serves an important rhetorical function, highlighting the completion of this sentence and beyond as the very words of YHWH, not the self-inspired utterance of a man with a personal vendetta (cf. Ezek 13:2 – 3).

By suspending the main clause Obadiah seizes the attention of hearers and readers, who wonder what he means by the ominous "on that day." But we do not wait long, for with brutal forthrightness YHWH announces the end of wisdom and understanding in Edom (v. 8c-d). The combination of verb הַאֲבִיד, "to destroy," and preposition מִן, "from," regularly means destruction and removal. The objects to be removed are identified in two sensitively cast parallel lines, with compensatory lengthening in the second line to restore balance, since the verb has been dropped:

| I-will-destroy | the wise | from Edom | a b c |
| And understanding | from Mount | Esau | b c¹ c² |

The features removed involve both concrete elements — "wise persons" (חֲכָמִים) — and the abstraction "wisdom" (lit., "understanding"; תְּבוּנָה) itself. References to Edom's wisdom occur elsewhere in the OT, most notably in Jer 49:7.[45] However, we

---

43. The present construction occurs elsewhere only in Ezek 38:14, but see also 24:25. On הֲלוֹא as an emphatic particle, see M. L. Brown, "'Is It Not??' or 'Indeed!': hᵃlōʾ in Northwest Semitic," *Maarav* 4 (1987): 201 – 19.

44. Watts, *Obadiah*, 35.

45. The book of Job has a pronounced Edomite flavor. Eliphaz, the leader of Job's three "friends," who speaks expressly of "wisdom" in 15:17 – 19, was from Teman (2:11). Job himself was from the land of Uz, apparently on the border of northern Arabia and southern Edom. See also Baruch 3:22 – 23.

should not interpret either Obadiah's or Jeremiah's statements to suggest that Edom was a hotbed of some sort of wisdom movement, such as is represented by Proverbs, Ecclesiastes, and Job in the Hebrew Bible. The issue in both these texts is the loss of counselors who may address the present national crisis and of wisdom to be applied to the crisis. In a sense, these statements clarify v. 7e: because YHWH has removed any who might have given counsel and the intelligence needed to produce wise counsel, they are at their wit's end.[46] Just as YHWH hardened Pharaoh's heart in the context of the exodus in order to achieve his intended result, so here he has removed those who might have sound solutions and the actual solutions to Esau's present crisis.

Verse 8c contains the second of only two references to Edom in Obadiah; here the prophet's focus is on the people represented by "Esau" rather than on the land. However, the expression "Mount Esau" in v. 8d (as well as vv. 9b, 19a, 21a) is striking. This phrase occurs only in Obadiah. When others refer to the mountainous region occupied by the descendants of Esau or their predecessors, they speak of Mount Seir,[47] or simply Seir.[48] Obadiah uses the present expression to keep the focus on the nation and to prepare for v. 10a, where Esau's fraternal relationship with Jacob is explicitly declared.

b. The effect of YHWH's action against Esau (v. 9). Needing another parallel expression for "Mount Esau," Obadiah now refers to "Teman." Although the genealogy of Edom in Gen 36 uses Teman as the personal name of Esau's grandson, Eliphaz' oldest son (Gen 36:11), and the gentilic "Temanites" in 36:34, when Teman is used as a proper noun elsewhere, it always names a place.[49] Its location is unknown, and though derived from a root יָמַן, meaning "south," this was probably a regional designation, referring perhaps to the northern part of Edom rather than to a town.[50]

The effect of YHWH's action on the land of Edom is twofold. First, panic will strike all the heroes of Teman. Here "your heroes" (גִּבּוֹרֶיךָ) refers to Teman's trained military forces, who will be paralyzed with fright.[51] Jeremiah 49:22 provides a vivid picture of Edom's fright on their "day" of doom: "The heart of the warriors of Edom in that day shall be like the heart of a woman in labor" (NRSV). Whether it is the announcement of Edom's doom that creates the panic or the "day" itself is not clear, but v. 9b declares the consequences of v. 9a;[52] the entire population will be annihilated. The passive יִכָּרֵת, "[he] will be cut off," leaves open the question who will cut off the population, though "I destroy" in v. 8c suggests YHWH is the primary agent.

Now we may look back and see how Obadiah has made his case, specifically highlighting the utter destruction of Esau. The victims of divine judgment include the wise, who should be finding solutions to the crisis, wisdom itself (i.e., the military who should be defending the nation against outsiders), and the entire population. Here אִישׁ, "a man," functions as a collective not only for the men of Edom, but all the Edomites.

c. The reason for YHWH's action against Esau (v. 10). Inasmuch as v. 10c and 10d are cast as parallel principal clauses, by definition they represent the center of gravity of this verse. In so doing they

46. Thus Renkema's rendering of v. 7e (*Obadiah*, 150).

47. Deut 1:2; 2:1, 5; Josh 15:10; 24:4; 2 Chr 20:23; Ezek 35:2, 3, 7, 15.

48. E.g., Deut 2:4, 8, 12, 22, 29.

49. Jer 49:7, 20; Ezek 25:13; Amos 1:12; Hab 3:3. Job 2:11 locates Eliphaz, the friend of Job, in Teman.

50. Cf. Amos 1:12, which speaks of the fire that YHWH hurls on Teman consuming the palaces of Bozrah. See further, E. A. Knauf, "Teman," *ABD*, 6:347 – 48.

51. Hebrew חָתַת means "to be emotionally shattered, to panic" (*HALOT*, 365 – 66). In Josh 10:25, Joshua used this verb (along with "do not fear," "be strong," and "be brave") to encourage his people.

52. On לְמַעַן introducing a result clause, see JM §169g.

continue to describe the effects of Esau's "day" on him.[53] Obadiah holds out no hope for him ever to be restored or revived. If v. 9a spoke of panic among the troops, now Obadiah deals with the social consequences for Esau as a whole of his elimination from the landscape: shame will cover him. In the OT this sort of shame has less to do with an internal conviction of guilt and unworthiness than with a loss of status and prestige; those who once enjoyed the respect of others have been disgraced and the respect is gone.[54] And how could it be otherwise, for Esau will be cut off forever?[55] In this instance Esau will wear this shame like a garment. This statement builds on v. 2, where YHWH had declared that he would make Esau small among the nations and held in extreme contempt. Obadiah hereby picks up on notions expressed even more vividly in Mic 7:10:

> Then my enemy will see [my vindication],
>> and shame will cover her who said to me,
>> "Where is the LORD your God?"

My eyes will see her downfall;
>> now she will be trodden down
>> like the mire of the streets. (NRSV)

If shame is not considered a sense of guilt or remorse but the loss of honor within the social context, we may understand how Esau could be covered with shame when he is gone. Obviously he could not feel these emotions, but in the eyes of the nations his standing has been totally destroyed.

But why should YHWH do this to Esau? Why create this contempt among the nations; and even more seriously, why impose the irreversible death penalty on him?[56] Until now Obadiah has been silent on Esau's crimes. Finally in v. 10a-b we get a hint — but it is only a fleeting hint, for at this point the prophet is still preoccupied with Esau's punishment. The crimes for which YHWH here accuses Esau are murder[57] and violence against his brother, Jacob.[58]

The word מִקָּטֶל is a hapax form from a rare root in Hebrew, קָטַל, "to kill."[59] The verb occurs

---

53. The second person masculine singular suffixes and verb forms continue.

54. See Jacqueline E. Lapsley, "Shame and Self-Knowledge: The Positive Role of Shame in Ezekiel's View of the Moral Self," in *The Book of Ezekiel: Theological and Anthropological Perspectives* (ed. by M. S. Odell and J. Strong; SBLSymS; Atlanta: Society of Biblical Literature, 2000), 143 – 73; Margaret S. Odell, "The Inversion of Shame and Forgiveness in Ezekiel 16.59 – 63," *JSOT* 56 (1992): 103. For a discussion of shame as a result of restoration, which functions quite differently, see now Eric Ortlund, "Shame in Restoration in Ezekiel," *Scandinavian Evangelical e-Journal* 2 (2011): 1 – 17.

55. Renkema (*Obadiah*, 161) renders וְנִכְרַתָּ, "and you will be cut off" as "and you will be counted as nothing." Similarly in v. 9b. The addition of לְעוֹלָם, "forever, in perpetuity," highlights the finality of YHWH's judgment. Cf. Jeremiah's emphatic statement, "Bozrah shall become an object of horror and ridicule, a waste, and an object of cursing; and all her towns shall be perpetual (עוֹלָם) wastes" (Jer 49:13 NRSV).

56. The niphal of כָּרַת, "to be cut off," followed by מִן "from" + social or geographic designation often refers to the death penalty: from one's people (Gen 17:14; Lev 7:20 – 27; etc.); from Israel (Exod 12:15; Num 19:13); from the congregation (Exod

12:19); from the midst of the assembly (Num 19:20); etc.

57. Most translations follow MT in interpreting מִקָּטֶל as the conclusion to v. 9, specifying the means by which YHWH cuts off Esau — through the actions of warriors. However, several considerations argue for attaching the word to v. 10: (1) Attaching the word to v. 9 is syntactically awkward. (2) The verb קָטַל, "to kill," is rare, occurring only three times in the OT, but always in the context of individual slaughter, never in a military context (Job 13:15; 24:14; Ps 139:19). In Job 24:14 it refers specifically to murder. (3) The ancient Greek and Latin versions place the word at the beginning of v. 10. (4) מִקָּטֶל is a natural correlative with מֵחֲמַס, "through violence," which follows. See further, Renkema, *Obadiah*, 156 – 58; Wolff, *Obadiah and Jonah*, 26 – 27, though Wolff interprets מֵחֲמַס as a gloss from Joel 4:19[3:19], which may originally have been a marginal note.

58. On the causative use of מִן, see JM§133e; GKC §119z.

59. This is an Aramaic loanword. See Dan 2:13, 14; 3:22; 5:19, 30; 7:11. For inscriptional attestation, see *DNWSI*, 1006 – 7. For discussion see Max Wagner, *Die Lexikalische Aramaismen im alttestamentlichen Hebrauisch* (BZAW 96; Berlin: Alfred Töpelmann, 1966), 254. In postbiblical Hebrew this word replaces הָרַג.

only three times, always with reference to killing a person (Ps 139:19; Job 13:15; 24:14). The Hebrew word חָמָס is a common expression in the OT, denoting a range of violent offenses, including emotional abuse (Gen 16:5), rape (Jer 13:22), abuse of the Torah (Ezek 22:26), abuse of the environment (Hab 2:17), exploitation of the socially marginalized (Amos 3:10), and murder (Gen 49:5 – 6). Here it serves as a catch-all term for violent action motivated by hatred and greed and lacking in any sympathy toward a victim. Behind this accusation we may hear Ezekiel's pronouncement of doom on Edom:

> Because you have harbored longstanding enmity, and handed the people of Israel over to the sword at the time of their calamity, the time of their final punishment — Therefore, by my life — the declaration of the Lord YHWH — surely, [it was] the blood of hatred, so blood will pursue you. (Ezek 35:5 – 6).[60]

However, the echoes of Joel 4:19[3:19] are even clearer:

> Egypt shall become a desolation
>   and Edom a desolate wilderness,
> because of the violence [מֵחֲמַס] done to the
>   people of Judah,
>   in whose land they have shed innocent blood.
>   (NRSV)

Obadiah identifies the victim of Esau's abuse as "your brother Jacob" (אָחִיךָ יַעֲקֹב). If the reader had any questions earlier about Obadiah's repeated use of the personal name Esau rather than the national or territorial designation, Edom, now those questions are answered. Keenly aware of the traditions of Esau and Jacob's birth and life in the household of Isaac, the prophet perceives the nations of Edom and Judah as brothers, descendants of a common father and mother. In contrast to the way Esau has treated Jacob, members of the same family should support and defend each other, especially in the face of threats from the outside.

However, as Amos had observed almost two centuries earlier, Esau had a history of stifling natural fraternal affections, allowing his rage to burn out of control and pursuing his brother with the sword (Amos 1:11 – 12). Indeed according to Amos's previous pronouncement against Tyre, the Edomites had forgotten their fraternal obligations,[61] and they willingly participated as accomplices in Tyre's slave trade; Amos intimates that the victims in this violent practice were his own brothers (Amos 1:9 – 10).

But Obadiah's charge is also reminiscent of Cain's crime against his brother Abel in Gen 4. Although the narrative uses different vocabulary, conceptually Esau's actions parallel those of Cain, who rose up against his brother and killed him (Gen 4:8). Cain's response to YHWH's question concerning the whereabouts of his brother is paradigmatic of Edom's response to Jacob: "Am I my brother's keeper?" (4:10). Both Cain and Esau answer this rhetorical question negatively, in direct contravention of natural filial affections and obligations. Because Jacob's blood cries out to YHWH from the ground (cf. 4:10b), YHWH must impose on him the death sentence. Remarkably, although YHWH in his grace had spared Cain, Obadiah holds out no such hope for Esau.

---

60. As translated by Daniel I. Block, *The Book of Ezekiel Chapters 25 – 48* (NICOT; Grand Rapids: Eerdmans, 1998), 310.

61. Hebrew בְּרִית אָחִים, "covenant of brothers/brotherhood."

Obadiah 11 – 14

C. The Indictment: *Esau's Crimes on the "Day of Jacob"*

Main Idea of the Passage

In presenting the indictment against Esau in this radically modified lawsuit, Obadiah recites the crimes for which he is condemned. He condemns Esau not only for gloating over the demise of his brother, but also for actively participating in his fall on "the day [of Jacob]."

Literary Context

Most prophetic judgment speeches follow typical court procedures, beginning with a summary of the charges against the accused and then announcing the divine sentence. Obadiah has reversed this order. Having begun his oracle proper by announcing Esau's doom (vv. 2 – 10), the prophet then justifies this with a recitation of Esau's crimes on "the day" of Jacob (vv. 11 – 14). However, in v. 10a-b he prepared for this phase by summarizing the charges against Esau. But the summary lacks detail and leaves hearers and readers wondering about the specific offenses that fall under the rubrics of "murder" (מִקְטֶל) and "violence" (חָמָס). Accordingly, vv. 11 – 14 function as a structural bridge between vv. 2 – 10 and vv. 15 – 21, setting the stage for the next phase (vv. 15 – 18), when we will learn more about the divine fury behind Esau's judgment.

Translation and Exegetical Outline

Obadiah 11–14

11a	בְּיוֹם עֲמָֽדְךָ מִנֶּגֶד	On the day that you stood aloof,
11b	בְּיוֹם שְׁבוֹת זָרִים חֵילוֹ	on the day that strangers carried off his nobility,
11c	וְנָכְרִים בָּאוּ (שְׁעָרָו) [שְׁעָרָיו]	and foreigners entered his gates,
11d	וְעַל־יְרוּשָׁלִַם יַדּוּ גוֹרָל	and for Jerusalem they cast lots,
11e	גַּם־אַתָּה כְּאַחַד מֵהֶם׃	you too were like one of them.
12a	וְאַל־תֵּרֶא בְיוֹם־אָחִיךָ	But you should not gloat over the day of your *brother*
12b	בְּיוֹם נָכְרוֹ	on the day of his misfortune.
12c	וְאַל־תִּשְׂמַח לִבְנֵי־יְהוּדָה	And you should not rejoice over the people of Judah
12d	בְּיוֹם אָבְדָם	on the day of their ruin.
12e	וְאַל־תַּגְדֵּל פִּיךָ	And you should not boast
12f	בְּיוֹם צָרָה׃	on the day of distress.
13a	אַל־תָּבוֹא בְשַׁעַר־עַמִּי	You should not enter the gate of my people
13b	בְּיוֹם אֵידָם	on the day of their doom.
13c	אַל־תֵּרֶא גַם־אַתָּה בְּרָעָתוֹ	You should not gloat — yes you — over his disaster
13d	בְּיוֹם אֵידוֹ	on the day of his doom.
13e	וְאַל־תִּשְׁלַחְנָה בְחֵילוֹ	And you should not reach for his wealth
14a	בְּיוֹם אֵידוֹ׃	on the day of his doom.
14b	וְאַל־תַּעֲמֹד עַל־הַפֶּרֶק	And you should not stand at the crossroads
14c	לְהַכְרִית אֶת־פְּלִיטָיו	to cut off his fugitives.
14d	וְאַל־תַּסְגֵּר שְׂרִידָיו	And you should not hand over his survivors
14e	בְּיוֹם צָרָה׃	on the day of distress.

C. The Indictment: Esau's Crimes on the "Day of Jacob" (vv. 11–14)

1. Esau's Actions against Jacob

2. Esau's Attitude toward Jacob

3. Esau's Actions against Jacob

Structure and Literary Form

Thematically and stylistically vv. 11 – 14 represent the most cohesive part of book. The beginning of the new subunit is signaled by בְּיוֹם עֲמָדְךָ, "on the day that you stood." That day in the past stands not only in opposition to the future day of Esau's judgment announced in v. 8a, but it also signals the theme of this segment. Indeed the word "day" (יוֹם) represents the key word, occurring a total of ten times in four verses.[1] Whereas the future day will be Esau's day of reckoning, as v. 12a suggests, the fateful day in the past may be identified as the "day [of Jacob]" (cf. 10a-b), the day when Judah, the last vestige of national Israel, experienced the violence of the nations. Verse 11 functions as a thematic statement, declaring in general terms Esau's misconduct on Jacob's day.

What follows consists of a series of eight charges cast according to a formulaic pattern involving "You should not" + verb + "on the day" + a descriptor of the day.[2] However, the pattern is broken in v. 14a-b, where, instead of referring to the "day," Obadiah adds a purpose clause. This modification not only focuses attention of this specific action, but after the opening statement in v. 10a, with the accusation that Esau "stood" (עָמַד) in opposition to his brother, the prophet has created an effective literary inclusio.

On another note, this segment is distinguished within the book for its apparent secularity. YHWH is never named, nor does he appear as the subject or object of any of the verbs. Indeed he is implicated only once in this entire section; in v. 13a Obadiah identifies the people of Judah (12c) as "my people" (עַמִּי). Otherwise the issues appear to be entirely between Esau and his brother. Our explanation of the text, particularly vv. 12 – 14 will be structured logically rather than line by line, considering first the characteristics of the "day [of Jacob]," and then the role that Esau played in making that day what it was for his brother.

Explanation of the Text

1. The Nature of the "Day of Jacob" (v. 11)

Although the subunit begins with a charge against Esau (v. 11a), the next three lines summarize the actions against Jerusalem committed by the nations in the context of the city's fall. The invaders are identified as "strangers" (זָרִים) and "foreigners" (נָכְרִים). In its most limited application, a זָר was an outsider to the household (Job 19:13 – 19), but it could also be used of laypersons in contrast to the priestly personnel. The present plural form often signifies strangers who are enemies of Israel.[3]

---

1. For similar repetitive style in Isaiah's portrayal of Judah's "day of reckoning," see Isa 2:12 – 17.

2. [וְ] + אַל + jussive verb + בְּיוֹם + descriptor.

3. Isa 1:7; 29:5; Jer 5:19; 30:8; 51:51; Ezek 7:21; 11:9; Hos 7:9; 8:7; Joel 4:17/[3:17]; specifically Babylon (Jer 51.2), Assyria (Ezek 31:12), Tyre (28:7, 10), Egypt (30:12). Occasional association with עָרִיצִים, "tyrants, usurpers," reflects violent overtones.

Fundamentally the root *nkr* speaks of being unknown, unrecognizable. The connotations of the Hebrew term are not as overtly hostile as the Akkadian cognate, *nakrum*, "enemy." Since a נָכְרִי could be anyone who is alien to the household (Job 19:15; Ps 69:9[8]; Prov 5:10), the present plural forms are often paired (cf. Lam 5:22).[4] Although everyone knows the invaders by name (Nebuchadnezzar and the Babylonians), by using these expressions Obadiah highlights Esau's unique status. He is neither a זָר nor a נָכְרִי, but a brother (אָח), who originated in the same household as Jacob, which intensifies the heinousness of his crimes against his brother.[5]

Obadiah identifies three specific actions that these aliens committed against Esau's brother, Jacob.[6] First, they carried off the significant members of the community. Although most English versions render חֵילוֹ in v. 11b as "his wealth," this interpretation is unlikely. The word can indeed mean wealth (Deut 8:18; etc.), but it bears a wide range of meanings, including "competence, power, faculty," "a military force, army," "a noble person or class of people."[7] The question is, Which sense suits the present context best? While the verb שָׁבָה may on rare occasions involve capturing and carrying off livestock (1 Chr 5:21) and other moveable property (2 Chr 21:17), in most instances it concerns the capture and deportation of human population.[8]

Admittedly, the narratives of the final fall of Jerusalem in 586 BC do not report the deportation of the upper classes. However the account of Nebuchadnezzar's earlier subjugation of the city in 598 BC highlights the deportation to Babylon of these people, including King Jehoiachin and his family (2 Kgs 24:14 – 16) and notes specifically that they

sent into exile "all the men of valor" (כָּל אַנְשֵׁי הַחַיִל, 24:16 NRSV). As Obadiah looks back on his own people's recent disasters, he appears to conflate the images of 598 and 586 BC, which may explain why he does not arrange the present three actions of the foreigners against Jerusalem in the logical order. The actual sequence would probably have involved entry into the city, deportation of the population, and casting lots for the city as spoil that remained.

Second, the foreigners entered Jacob's gates (v. 11c). The word שְׁעָרִים refers fundamentally to gate structures that were part of the defensive walls around a settlement. For foreigners to enter the gates means that the defensive walls, equipment, and strategies have failed. Because the word was also used as a synechdoche (figure of speech) for the space within the walls (Deut 5:14; 12:12; 14:21, 27), the present action involves more than entering the gates; it means entering the gates and taking over the town, which typically involved violent actions like raping the women, slaughtering the men, and pillaging and ransacking the place (cf. v. 6a-b). This event is commemorated in Lam 4:12, though here the poet uses much stronger language for the invader:

> The kings of the earth did not believe,
>   nor did any of the inhabitants of the world,
>   that foe [צָר] or enemy [אוֹיֵב] could enter
>   the gates of Jerusalem. (NRSV)

Third, "they cast lots" for Jerusalem. In the ancient world it was common for conquerors to cast lots for the loot they had won. The distribution of the territories among the twelve tribes of Israel in Josh 15 – 19 and the allocation of cities to the Levites in Josh 21 symbolized the Israelites' victory over the Canaanites. The images of casting lots for the

---

4. For further discussion of these terms, see Daniel I. Block, "Sojourner; Alien; Stranger," *ISBE*, rev. ed., 4:562 – 63.

5. Cf. Deut 17:15, which expressly contrasts a נָכְרִי, "foreigner," with an אָח, "brother."

6. The antecedent for the third person suffix on חֵילוֹ in v. 11b is "your brother Jacob" in v. 10b.

7. For references, see *HALOT*, 311 – 12.

8. Deut 21:10; Judg 5:12; 1 Kgs 8:46 – 48, 50; 2 Kgs 6:22; Jer 41:10, 14; etc.

population generally in Joel 4:3[3:3] — associated with trading boys and selling girls — and for the nobles (נְכָדִים) in Nah 3:10 are more natural than casting lots for the city. The action could have served several different functions: (1) to divide Jerusalem into regions, which were then assigned to contingents of Babylonian troops to administer and control; (2) to determine what was to be taken as booty and what was to be destroyed; or (3) to determine which part of the population was to be deported and which part was allowed to remain to serve those who occupied the city or to work the vineyards and fields (Jer 39:10).

In vv. 12 – 14 Obadiah describes the effects of these actions on Jerusalem. Whereas in v. 11a-d he had described that event as the day when Esau "stood aloof" and when foreigners captured the city, now in v. 12a he identifies it as "the day of your brother" (יוֹם אָחִיךָ). The expression "day of your brother" recalls the reference to "your brother Jacob" in v. 10b and designates the fall of Jerusalem as "the day of Jacob." The present expression is equivalent to "the day of Jerusalem" in Ps 137:7. Obadiah describes the effect of the "day" of Jacob's brother with a series of modifiers:

v. 12b the day of his misfortune (יוֹם נָכְרוֹ)
v. 12d the day of their ruin (יוֹם אָבְדָם)
v. 12f the day of distress (יוֹם צָרָה)
v. 13b the day of their doom (יוֹם אֵידָם)
v. 13d the day of his doom (יוֹם אֵידוֹ)

v. 13f the day of his doom (יוֹם אֵידוֹ)
v. 14d the day of distress (יוֹם צָרָה)

In addition, in v. 13c the prophet speaks of "[the time of] his disaster" (בְּרָעָתוֹ).

The first expression (v. 12b) (יוֹם נָכְרוֹ) involves a hapax form, נֵכֶר, which obviously derives from the same root as נָכְרִי, "foreigner," in v. 11c, suggesting something like "day of his foreignness,"[9] perhaps because he became a foreigner to his brother Esau, or the day he became a foreigner to himself.[10] Alternatively, since this is a hapax, it is possible that נָכְרוֹ should be linked with Akkadian *nakrum*, "enemy,"[11] a much more negative expression than נָכְרִי in Hebrew. Accordingly, "the day of his enemy" refers to the day the enemy intervened in Jacob's history and determined his fate — like "the day of YHWH" will be for Edom in v. 15a.

The second expression, יוֹם אָבְדָם, "day of their ruin," involves the same root as in v. 8c, where YHWH had said he would destroy the wise from Edom. The plural suffix is necessitated by "the people of Judah" in v. 12c.

Variations of the third, יוֹם צָרָה, which is repeated in v. 14d, occur twenty-five times in the OT.[12] The association with other expressions suggests צָרָה may refer to any experience that caused stress and anxiety.

The fourth word, אֵיד, occurs three times in v. 13 and almost two dozen times elsewhere in the OT.[13] While the etymology of אֵיד is uncertain,[14]

---

9. Cf. LXX, ἐν ἡμέρα ἀλλοτρίων, "in the day of foreigners"; Vulgate, *in die peregrinationis*, "in the day of his travel," i.e., exile.

10. Cf. Deut 4:27 – 28, according to which because of persistent rebellion YHWH would scatter Israel among the peoples, where they could serve alien gods all they wanted.

11. *CAD* 11.192 – 95.

12. Variations of יוֹם צָרָה, "day of distress/trouble: Gen 35:3; 2 Kgs 19:3 = Is 37:3; Pss 20:2[1]; 50:15; 59:16; 77:3[2]; 86:7; Prov 24:10; 25:19; Jer 16:19; Obad 12, 14; Nah 1:7; Hab 3:16; Zeph 1:15; of עֵת צָרָה, "time of distress/trouble): Judg 10:14; 2 Chr

28:22; Neh 9:27; Ps 37:39; Isa 33:2; Jer 14:8; 15:11; 30:7; Dan 12:1.

13. "Day" and "doom" (אֵד + יוֹם) are combined elsewhere in 2 Sam 22:19 = Ps 18:19[18], Jer 18:17; and Prov 27:10. In Jeremiah אֵיד expresses Yahweh's judgmental activity (Jer 18:17; 46:21; 48:16; cf. Deut 32:35); in Ps 18:19[18] (= 2 Sam 22:19) it represents the antithesis to divine aid and salvation.

14. P. K. McCarter ("The River Ordeal in Israelite Literature," *HTR* 66 [1973]: 403 – 12) suggests it is a loanword from Sumerian *id*, via Akkadian. In Mesopotamian texts the divine River *id* declares innocent a person who, in the context of "trial by ordeal," has been thrown into the river but has survived.

its meaning is clarified in Ezek 35:5, which pairs the expression עֵת אֵיד, "the time of doom," with עֵת עֲוֺן קֵץ, "the time of their final punishment." In the present context the first occurrence has the plural suffix, "their doom," presumably under the influence of "my people" (עַמִּי) in v. 13a, and the other two have the singular suffix, "his doom." If this oracle ever reached the Edomites, the ring of the first would have been ominous.[15] Remarkably, of the four occurrences of the word relating to the fall of Jerusalem, three are found in oracles against Edom.[16] Taken together these expressions paint an extremely dark picture of Jerusalem's final days.

2. Esau's Response to the "Day of Jacob" (vv. 12 – 13)

Despite the graphic description of the foreigners' actions on the day of Jacob in v. 11b-d, Obadiah's bitterness is not so much over the actions of the foreigners who invaded Judah — which explains why he refers to them with relatively innocuous expressions ("strangers" and "foreigners," rather than "foes" and "enemies") — as over Esau, who is not a foreigner but Jacob's own brother. Instead of defending a family member in time of crisis, Esau had stood by aloof and watched while the enemies destroyed the city (v. 11a). The idiom "to stand aloof" (עָמַד מִנֶּגֶד)[17] could mean either standing by and watching indifferently, or standing by as spectators at a sports event and cheering on the antagonists.

The latter image is suggested by Ps 137:7, which portrays the Edomites encouraging the Babylonians with "Raze it! Raze it! To its very foundations!"

While at first sight the opening line of Obad 11 suggests a certain passivity on the part of Esau with reference to Jacob, v. 11e paints a different picture. The construction of the verse as a whole and the word order of this line in particular signal the climax. The sense of גַּם אַתָּה כְּאַחַד מֵהֶם may be captured with "Yes! You too were like one of them!"[18] And this is what energizes the prophet throughout the book. Far from standing up to the invaders, Esau either tacitly or actually joined them in their violence against his own brother. From Jeremiah and Ezekiel it is clear that Babylon was the primary agent sent by YHWH to execute his judgments on his own people for centuries of infidelity and apostasy; for Esau to have joined them was unconscionable. This was more than a crime against humanity; it was a crime against one's own family. Esau the brother had become Esau the enemy![19]

If the prophet has previously only spoken in general terms of the involvement of Esau in the last days of the kingdom of Judah and of her capital city, Jerusalem, his approach changes dramatically in vv. 12 – 14, as he presents a litany of ways in which Esau proved Obadiah was just like the nations that had invaded Jerusalem. With impressive rhetorical force he exposes the crimes of Esau with a series of prohibitions, cast according to a formulaic pattern: "You should not" (אַל) + verb.[20]

---

15. Compare the vocalization of Edom (אֱדוֹם) and אָדָם.

16. Obad 13; also Jer 49:8; Ezek 35:5; cf. Jer 49:32, which concerns "Kedar and the kingdoms of Hazor."

17. For a variation of the idiom, see הִתְיַצֵּב מִנֶּגֶב in 2 Sam 18:13, where an unnamed man speaks of Joab standing aside/aloof, not getting involved.

18. On the emphatic function of גַּם, see T. Muraoka, *Emphatic Words and Structures in Biblical Hebrew* (Leiden: Brill, 1985), 143 – 46. On the focusing function of the particle (a "focus inducing connector," 199), see C. H. J. van der Merwe, *The Old Hebrew Particle gam: A Syntactic-semantic Description*

of gam in Gn – 2Kg (Münchener Universitätsschriften; St. Ottilien: EOS Verlag Erzabtei, 1990; idem, "Old Hebrew Particles and the Interpretation of Old Testament Texts," *JSOT* 60 (1993): 35 – 38. The construction as a verbless clause rather than a verbal statement (e.g., "You acted just like one of them") suggests a timeless significance: it was true in the past, and it continues to be so. Cf. Raabe, *Obadiah*, 176.

19. Cf. Renkema, *Obadiah*, 170.

20. אַל[וֹ] + jussive verb + בְּיוֹם + descriptor. The first three and the last three begin with the *waw* conjunction, distinguishing them from the middle two, which lack it.

Although he cites eight reasons why YHWH is justified in pouring out his wrath on Esau, the change in form in the seventh signals the climax of this litany of crimes. Instead of following up the prohibition (v. 14a) with a reference to "the day," as he does in all the others, Obadiah inserts a purpose clause: "to cut off his fugitives" (v. 14b).

It is generally acknowledged that in the OT the number seven symbolizes completeness and perfection.[21] The symbolic significance of the number eight is less obvious, but one could perhaps interpret it as reinforcing the perfection.[22] Whether or not this is correct, the 1 + 7 or 7 + 1 combinations that occur are striking. Israel's religious calendar was framed by two eight-day festivals. The spring festivals followed the 1 + 7 pattern, with Passover being celebrated on Nisan 14 (Exod 12:6, 18; Lev 23:5; Num 9:1 – 9; 28:16; etc.), to be followed by the seven-day Festival of Unleavened Bread, which concluded on the twenty-first day (Exod 12:15 – 20; Deut 16:1 – 8).

However, the 7 + 1 pattern is more common. In the autumn the Festival of Booths (Sukkoth) was to be celebrated for a week, beginning on Tishri 15, but it was to be followed by an eighth holy day marked by special offerings (אֲצֶרֶת) and total abstention from work (Lev 23:34 – 38). Jesse had 7 + 1 sons, the eighth being the divinely chosen king of Israel (1 Sam 16:6 – 13; 17:12). Since the seventh

in the present series is specially marked syntactically, we may recognize here another example of the 7 + 1 pattern. Although the opening formula is missing, Obadiah has hereby doubled the formula with which Amos opened all his oracles against the nations, including his pronouncement against Edom (Amos 1:11): "For three crimes of X, even for four, I will not revoke [the punishment]."[23] In effect this prophet seems to be saying, "For seven crimes of Esau, even for eight I will not revoke [the punishment]." However, whereas Amos only cites the fourth charge, Obadiah lists all eight.[24] Speaking on behalf of YHWH, the prophet shouts out his indignation over the crimes Esau has committed against his brother.

However, one question remains: How shall we understand the negative particle (אַל) followed by jussive verbs? Normally this construction involves prohibition of future actions. However, if our interpretation of the context for Obadiah's ministry is correct, this makes no sense, since the atrocities involve past actions.[25] This is how NRSV renders these verbs ("you should not have …"), but this seems grammatically untenable. Some interpret the jussives as imaginative interpretations of past actions as if they were present or future.[26] It seems best, however, to let the jussives bear their normal incompleted sense: not to treat these as allusions

21. Note the seven days of creation (Gen 1:1 – 2:4a), the seven speeches of YHWH by which he instructs the Israelites in the construction of the tabernacle (Exod 25 – 31), the seven pillars on which Lady Wisdom builds her house (Prov 9:1); Job's family consisting of seven sons and three daughters (Job 42:13).

22. Male children were circumcised on the eighth day as a seal of membership in the covenant community (Gen. 17:12; Lev. 12:3), and Nazirites were purified on the eighth day (Num 6:10); after Hezekiah's men had cleansed the temple they consecrated the temple in two eight-day phases (2 Chr 29:17).

23. Cf. Amos 1:3, 6, 9, 13; 2:1, 4, 6.

24. For other illustrations of this sort of numerical rhetoric, see Prov 6:16 – 19[6 even 7]; 30:18 – 31[3 even 4]. In 30:11 – 14

the sage lists four types of people, which presumably belong to the same class of sayings, though lacking the opening formula.

25. This grammatical form provides the strongest argument for a preexilic date for the book. See Niehaus, "Obadiah," 497. However the argument works with equal force against the preexilic date; v. 11a-e uses perfect forms, which normally refer to past actions — unless of course these perfects refer to the vision that occurred in the prophet's past and not the events. Cf. Rogland, *Alleged Non-Past Uses of* Qatal *in Classical Hebrew*, 69 – 70.

26. Allen, *Joel, Obadiah, Jonah, and Micah*, 156. This solution reverses the treatment of prophetic perfects, which view future actions as so certain or imminent they may be spoken of as already transpired.

to past actions, but as prohibitions with ongoing force — not only for Edom, but for everyone else, including the hearers/readers of the prophet's oracle. No one should treat a sibling the way Esau has treated Jacob. Our translation above seeks to capture this sense. Esau's crimes against Jacob are listed as follows:

1. He gloated (רָעָה) over the day of his brother (v. 12a).
2. He celebrated (שָׂמַח) over his ruin (v. 12c).
3. He boasted (הִגְדִּיל פֶּה) when Jacob fell (v. 12e).
4. He invaded (בּוֹא) the sacred city of YHWH's people (v. 13a).
5. He gloated (רָעָה) over Jacob's calamity (v. 13e).
6. He claimed (שָׁלַח) Jacob's property (v. 13f).
7. He cut off (כָּרַת) the fugitives of Jacob (v. 14a).
8. He handed over (הִסְגִּיר) the survivors of Jacob over to the enemies (v. 14c).

Based on their content and style, this list divides generally into two segments, the first of which (v. 12) focuses on Esau's attitude toward Jacob's demise, and the second on his active participation therein (vv. 13 – 14), though the division is not absolute. The idiom רָאָה בְ, "to look on" (##1, 5), refers to gazing intently at or gloating over a scene, in this case the day of Jacob his brother, that is, the doom of Judah/Jerusalem.[27] This understanding is reinforced by the second prohibition, which speaks of rejoicing over Jacob's demise (cf. Ezek 35:15; 36:5; Lam 4:21). In a sense, because this crime goes against natural affections, it is worse than rejoicing over the extinction of one's enemy referred to frequently elsewhere.[28] The image is concretized in the third prohibition, which speaks of Esau literally

"making his mouth big." The idiom used here, הִגְדִּיל פֶּה, occurs elsewhere only in Ezekiel's oracle against Edom (Ezek 35:13), where the bragging involves claiming Israel and Judah and their lands as their own (35:10). Since these lands have been given over to them, they may devour them if they so choose (35:12). However, in Ezekiel the braggadocio is directed against YHWH ("against me"; עָלַי, 35:13).

The fourth prohibition notes that Esau followed the foreigners into Jerusalem (cf. v. 11c), which was the city of YHWH's people. Obadiah's use of the expression עַמִּי is remarkable not only because it breaks up a text that otherwise looks like it involves only two brothers with a reference to YHWH, but especially because of the hope it offers. Jerusalem and the land are significant to YHWH because they represent the other two apexes of the eternal covenantal triangle that he had established long ago (see Fig. 3.1). By inserting the phrase "my people," the prophet suggests that although the events of 586 BC signaled divorce among all these parties and the suspension of the benefits of covenant relationship, in YHWH's eyes Israel still was — and would always be — his covenant people.[29]

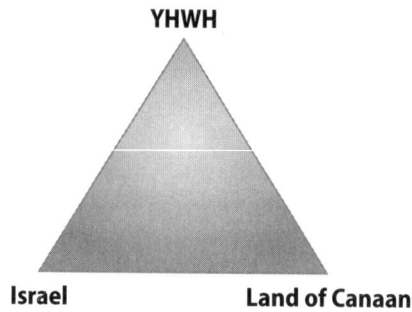

Figure 3.1: The Covenantal Triangle

---

27. With delight (Eccl 2:1); with grief (Gen 21:16; 44:34; Esth 8:6); with compassion (Gen 29:32; 1Sam 1:11; Ps 106:44); with curiosity (1 Sam 6:19); with sadistic glee (*Schadenfreude*; Pss 22:18[17]; 37:34; 54:9[7]; 112:8).

28. Job 31:29; Prov 24:17 – 18; Pss 35:19 – 24; 38:17[16] (cf. Ezek 25:6).

29. Should we hear here an echo and reversal of Hos 1 – 2, where YHWH had reversed Israel's previous standing with him: "my people" (עַמִּי) had become "not my people" (לֹא עַמִּי). See Hos 1:9.

The sixth prohibition involves an elliptical expression. Normally the idiom for "to grasp, seize" would be "to stretch out the hand against/for" (שָׁלַח יָד). However, there is no need to insert "your hand" into the text, since this elliptical form of the idiom is attested elsewhere. But for what did Esau grasp? In contrast to v. 11b, where חַיִל had referred to the nobility among the people, here the same word is used of property, that is, the lot belonging to Jacob that Esau would claim.[30]

As observed above, the form of the seventh prohibition (v. 14a-b) differs from the rest, which suggests this entry marks a climax or focus to the entire list. In v. 11a we learned that on the day of Jacob Esau had stood (עָמַד) aloof while Jerusalem burned. But now we discover that this was not the only place where he was standing. He also stood in the way at the entrances to Judah's escape routes. Whatever the etymology of the rare word פֶּרֶק, given the reference to פְּלִיטִים, "fugitives," in v. 14b, this undoubtedly refers to routes the people from Judah and Jerusalem used to escape the horrors of captivity at the hands of foreigners and the routes to refuge in the land of Jacob's brother. However, instead of offering them sanctuary, Esau cut off the escapees.[31] In view of v. 14c-d we might have expected some word for "capture." Instead in this climactic statement, Obadiah uses a much stronger

expression. Like Cain, Esau does not shrink back from murdering his brother.

This interpretation is reinforced by the last prohibition, which insists that people should never hand over their brothers to the enemy. The expression הִסְגִּיר, "to hand over," involves one person who has control over another transferring that person into the hands of another person.[32] The word שְׂרִידָיו, "his survivors," refers to those who survived the disasters associated with the fall of Jerusalem (cf. v. 18f). Singular and plural forms of this word form a natural pair with the counterparts of פָּלִיט, "fugitive," not only here but elsewhere.[33] Presumably the survivors here are not the escapees spoken of in v. 14b, who have sought refuge in Edom, but survivors within the land who have fallen into the hands of Edomites. With respect to the day of YHWH in Jerusalem, Lam 2:22 declares, "On the day of the anger of YHWH no one escaped [פָּלִיט] or survived [שָׂרִיד]; those whom I bore and raised my enemy destroyed."

With this the indictment of Esau concludes. If YHWH pours out his wrath on him, this is certainly neither a reflection of divine petulance nor playing favorites unconditionally with Jacob. On the contrary, Jacob has paid for his sins; now Esau must do the same.

---

30. The word is often used this way. See Gen 34:29; Num 31:9; Deut 8:17; Isa 8:4; 10:14; Jer 15:13; etc.

31. The sense of "cut off" the escape route is unlikely, since the hiphil form הִכְרִית is never used this way.

32. While the element is missing here, it often occurs with "into the hands of X": Josh 20:5; 1 Sam 23:11 – 12, 20; 30:15; Ps 31:10[9]; Lam 2:7. Cf. with לְ, "to," someone, see Amos 1:6, 9; Ps 78:48, 50, 62; with אֶל, Deut 23:15[16]; Job 16:11. How common

the notion was in the ANE is reflected in the early fifth-century sarcophagus inscription of Eshmunazar, king of Sidon. As part of a curse invoked on anyone who would disturb the corpse of the king, he has inscribed, "May the holy gods deliver him (ויסגרנם) up to a mighty ruler who shall hold sway over him to bring an end to him." COS 2.57, lines 9 – 10, as translated by P. K. McCarter (p. 183).

33. Josh 8:22; Jer 42:17; 44:14; Lam 2:22.

Obadiah 15 – 18

D. The Bad Good News:
The Demise of Esau on the "Day of YHWH"

Main Idea of the Passage

Obadiah announces the imminence of "the day of YHWH" for the nations. YHWH's treatment of Esau becomes paradigmatic of YHWH's treatment of all who have stood in opposition to him and his people. At the same time he offers hope for Israel, promising the survivors of their own day restoration to himself and to the land.

Literary Context

Having announced Esau's day of judgment (vv. 2b – 10d) and justified it by reciting his crimes against his brother on "the day [of Jacob]" (vv. 11 – 14), the attention shifts to the future day of judgment as "the day of YHWH." But v. 15b-c links this paragraph tightly to what has preceded, announcing that the retributive principle of divine justice will be applied to Esau. However, Esau will not be the only target of divine wrath on that day; the nations are also on YHWH's radar. In v. 16 the role of the nations has obviously shifted from v. 1c-f, where they were drawn into Esau's day as agents of divine judgment. Verses 17a – 18e are transitional, anticipating Israel's ultimate restoration, a theme declared more explicitly in vv. 19 – 21.

A. Introduction: Setting the Stage for the "Days" (v. 1)

B. The Judgment: Esau's Humiliation on His "Day" of Doom (vv. 2 – 10)

C. The Indictment: Esau's Crimes on the "Day of Jacob" (vv. 11 – 14)

→ **D. The Bad Good News: The Demise of Esau on the "Day of YHWH" (vv. 15 – 18)**

E. The Good Good News: The Restoration of Jacob on the "Day of YHWH" (vv. 19 – 21)

Translation and Exegetical Outline

Obadiah 15–18

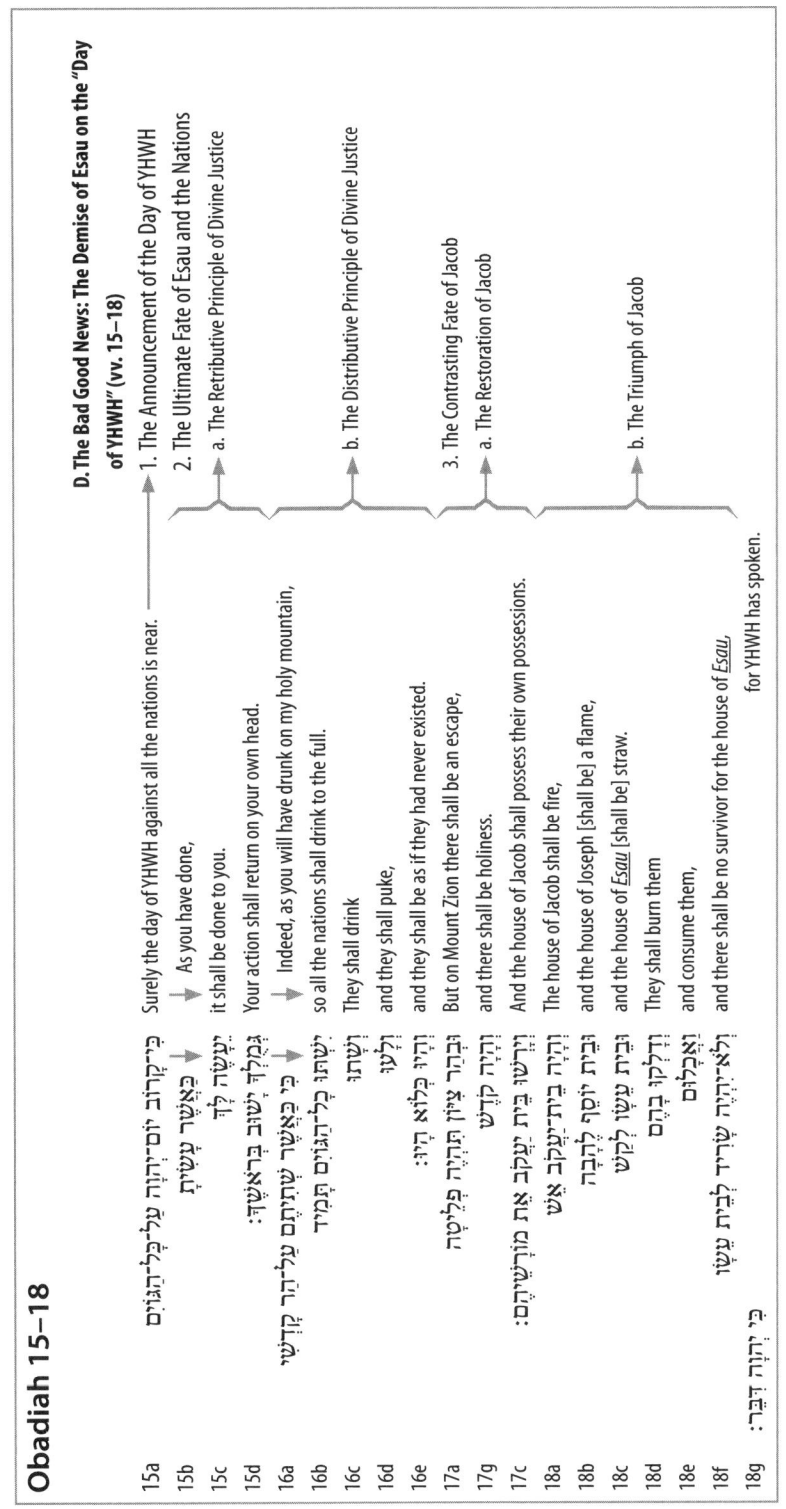

D. The Bad Good News: The Demise of Esau on the "Day of YHWH" (vv. 15–18)

1. The Announcement of the Day of YHWH
2. The Ultimate Fate of Esau and the Nations
   a. The Retributive Principle of Divine Justice
   b. The Distributive Principle of Divine Justice
3. The Contrasting Fate of Jacob
   a. The Restoration of Jacob
   b. The Triumph of Jacob

15a Surely the day of YHWH against all the nations is near.
15b As you have done,
15c it shall be done to you.
15d Your action shall return on your own head.
16a Indeed, as you will have drunk on my holy mountain,
16b so all the nations shall drink to the full.
16c They shall drink
16d and they shall puke,
16e and they shall be as if they had never existed.
17a But on Mount Zion there shall be an escape,
17g and there shall be holiness.
17c And the house of Jacob shall possess their own possessions.
18a The house of Jacob shall be fire,
18b and the house of Joseph [shall be] a flame,
18c and the house of *Esau* [shall be] straw.
18d They shall burn them
18e and consume them,
18f and there shall be no survivor for the house of *Esau*,
18g for YHWH has spoken.

Structure and Literary Form

The particle כִּי in v. 15a signals the commencement of a new segment of this prophecy. Most translations render the word causally ("For"),[1] as if the notice of the imminent day of YHWH should motivate a change in Esau's behavior. However, as noted earlier, the immanence of the day of YHWH can scarcely be motivation for Esau's past behavior. Accordingly, כִּי should be interpreted as deictic focusing particle ("surely"), marking the climax or peak of the composition.[2] Although Obadiah has spent considerable time speaking of the "day of Esau" and the "day of Jacob," this has all been preamble to the ultimate day, "the day of YHWH." Inasmuch as vv. 19 – 21 continue the portrayal of that day, v. 15a functions as a thesis statement for the remainder of the book. However, this larger segment (vv. 15 – 21) is split into two by the declarative prophetic formula, "for YHWH has spoken" in v. 18g, which suggests vv. 15 – 18 should be treated as a subsection.

On the surface, the material between these framing elements seems disparate, involving (in order) Esau (v. 15b-c), the nations (v. 16), and the house of Jacob (vv. 17 – 18). This has led many to treat v. 15b-c as the conclusion to vv. 11a-d, and they attach v. 15a directly to v. 16.[3] However, not only is this rearrangement without manuscript support, but it also affects the rhetoric of this section significantly. It obscures (1) Esau's fate as paradigmatic for the fate of the nations; (2) the noticeable shift from retributive to distributive justice in vv. 15b – 16e;[4] (3) the progression in focus from Esau to the nations to Jacob; (4) the impressive inclusio involving Esau at the beginning (v. 15b-c) and at the end (v. 18) — probably alluding to the burning of Jerusalem in 586 BC, with the latter concretizing the former; and (5) the bifold nature of the "day of YHWH."

YHWH's active defense of righteousness on behalf of his people on that day involves both judgment of the wicked (Esau) and vindication of his irrevocable covenant commitment to his people (Jacob). Indeed the present structure highlights the (ironic) reversals, placing the restoration of Jacob as the people of YHWH squarely within the context of the outpouring of divine wrath on the one people who should have stood by their brother on that earlier "day of YHWH." Despite the brief shift to the nations in v. 16, the focus remains on Esau until the end of the book.

1. So also Raabe, *Obadiah*, 190; Ben Zvi, *Obadiah,*169.
2. Similarly Wolff, *Obadiah and Jonah*, 62; Wendland, "Obadiah's 'Day,'" 36; Renkema, *Obadiah*, 185. On this use of כִּי, see the detailed study of Follingstad, *Deictic Viewpoint in Biblical Hebrew Text*, 52. For discussion of the similar function of this particle in Ps 38:19[18], see Lunn, *Word-Order Variation in Biblical Hebrew Poetry*, 170 – 71.
3. See above, p. 45.
4. So also Niehaus, "Obadiah," 536.

Explanation of the Text

1. The Announcement of the Day of YHWH (v. 15a)

Obadiah begins the second major section of his prophecy by announcing a familiar theme: the imminence of "the day of YHWH." Whether or not he coined the phrase, in the OT Amos was the first person to use the expression יוֹם יהוה:

> Woe to you who desire the day of YHWH!
> Why do you wish for the day of YHWH?
> It is darkness, not light
> as if someone fled from a lion, and was met by a bear;
> or went into the house and rested a hand against the wall,
> and was bitten by a snake.
> Is not the day of YHWH darkness, rather than light,
> and gloom with no brightness in it?
>
> (Amos 5:18 – 20)

By the time of Obadiah, יוֹם יהוה had become a stereotypical expression for the future moment when YHWH would personally break into human history, intervening with perfect righteousness on behalf of his people, lavishing his blessing on them, defeating their enemies, and setting his people high above the nations — in accordance with the ancient promises (Deut 28:1 – 13a).[5]

In this phrase יוֹם obviously does not refer to a twenty-four-hour period, but a moment/event in time, without reference to duration. As Amos had warned and as the people of Israel and Judah had experienced in 722 and 586 BC, the phrase "day of YHWH" refers to the moment of YHWH's intervention in history, whether for good or for ill. Zephaniah, who provides the most detailed description of the horrors of that day for Jerusalem, envisions the "day of YHWH" as a "day of YHWH's wrath" (עֶבְרָה; Zeph 1:18; cf. Ezek. 7:19), and the "day of YHWH's fury" (אַף; Zeph 2:2, 3). Lamentations 2:22 adds that there was no escapee (פָּלִיט) or survivor (שָׂרִיד). Since these oracles were delivered before Obadiah, we may reasonably assume that our prophet was familiar with these words and that he deliberately borrowed from this tradition to predict the demise of Esau and the nations.

Although many understand the "day of YHWH" as an eschatological expression referring to some event in the distant future, it is clear from Obadiah's announcement of the day that his focus is on its nearness (קָרוֹב).[6] Some of his predecessors cynically assumed the day would not happen for a long time (Isa 13:22; Ezek 12:22, 25, 27), despite the prophets' warnings that the day was "near" (קָרוֹב),[7] would happen shortly (Zeph 1:14; cf. Jer 48:16), and was "coming" (בָּא).[8] Indeed Obadiah's own generation had witnessed the fulfillment of these

---

5. The expression occurs elsewhere in Isa 13:6, 9; Ezek 13:5; Joel 1:15; 2:1, 11; 3:4[2:31]; 4:14[3:14]; Amos 5:18a, 18b, 20; Zeph 1:7, 14a, 14b; Mal 3:23[4:5]. Related references to YHWH's day occur in Isa 2:12 (against the arrogant); 22:5 (of tumult and trampling and chaos); 34:8 and 63:4 (of vengeance); Jer 46:10 (of vengeance); Ezek 30:3 (of cloud [and doom] for the nations); Zech 14:1.

6. Hebrew קָרוֹב יוֹם יהוה עַל כָּל הַגּוֹיִם, "Near is the day of YHWH against all nations," follows the normal P-S order of

verbless clauses of classification (Francis I. Anderson, *The Hebrew Verbless Clause in the Pentateuch* [JBL Monograph Series 14; Nashville: Abingdon, 1970], 42 – 45). Whereas in the past this P-S structure was viewed to be emphatic, here it is more a matter of focus than emphasis.

7. See Isa 13:6; Ezek 30:3; Joel 1:15; 2:1; 4:14[3:14]; Zeph 1:7, 14.

8. See Isa 13:9; Ezek 7:7; Joel 2:1; cf. plural "days are coming" Isa 39:6; Jer 7:32; 9:24[25]; 19:6; Amos 4:2; 8:11.

Zephaniah 1:7 – 18

⁷For the day of the Lᴏʀᴅ is at hand;
the Lᴏʀᴅ has prepared a sacrifice,
     he has consecrated his guests.
⁸And on the day of the Lᴏʀᴅ's sacrifice
     I will punish the officials and the king's sons
     and all who dress themselves in foreign attire.
⁹On that day I will punish
     all who leap over the threshold,
who fill their master's house
     with violence and fraud.
¹⁰On that day, says the Lᴏʀᴅ,
     a cry will be heard from the Fish Gate,
a wail from the Second Quarter,
     a loud crash from the hills.
¹¹The inhabitants of the Mortar wail,
     for all the traders have perished;
     all who weigh out silver are cut off.
¹²At that time I will search Jerusalem with lamps,
     and I will punish the people
who rest complacently on their dregs,
     those who say in their hearts,
"The Lᴏʀᴅ will not do good,
     nor will he do harm."
¹³Their wealth shall be plundered,
     and their houses laid waste.
Though they build houses,
     they shall not inhabit them;

though they plant vineyards,
     they shall not drink wine from them.
¹⁴The great day of the Lᴏʀᴅ is near,
     near and hastening fast;
the sound of the day of the Lᴏʀᴅ is bitter,
     the warrior cries aloud there.
¹⁵That day will be a day of wrath,
     a day of distress and anguish,
a day of ruin and devastation,
     a day of darkness and gloom,
a day of clouds and thick darkness,
     ¹⁶a day of trumpet blast and battle cry
against the fortified cities
     and against the lofty battlements.
¹⁷I will bring such distress upon people
     that they shall walk like the blind;
     because they have sinned against the Lᴏʀᴅ,
their blood shall be poured out like dust,
     and their flesh like dung.
¹⁸Neither their silver nor their gold
     will be able to save them
     on the day of the Lᴏʀᴅ's wrath;
in the fire of his passion
     the whole earth shall be consumed;
for a full, a terrible end he will make
     of all the inhabitants of the earth.

(Zeph 1:7 – 18, NRSV)

predictions and had felt the full force of YHWH's fury. However, with Obadiah's last phrase "against all the nations" (עַל כָּל הַגּוֹיִם), he announces that what had happened to Israel would soon happen to their enemies.⁹ In transferring the divine fury to

Israel's and Judah's enemies, Obadiah affirms what earlier prophets had predicted¹⁰ and seems to see the imminent day as the fulfillment of YHWH's own declaration in Israel's national anthem many centuries earlier in Deut 32:35:

---

9. On "the day" being "against" (עַל) someone, see Zeph 1:16.

10. All nations (Joel 3:4[2:31]; 4:14[3:14]); Babylon (Isa

13:6; Jer 51:47, 52); Egypt (Jer 46:10; Ezek 30:3); Philistines and Phoenicians (Jer 47:4); Edom (Isa 34:8); Moab (Jer 48:12); Bene Ammon (Jer 49:2); Gog (Ezek 39:8).

Vengeance is mine, and recompense,

for the time when their foot shall slip;

because the day of their calamity [יוֹם אֵידָם] is at hand,

their doom comes swiftly. (NRSV)

There is urgency in Obadiah's announcement about the coming day of YHWH against the nations, but it is driven far less by a concern for Esau to repent and change his ways[11] than to inspire hope in his own people. As with other prophets' oracles against foreign nations (e.g., Ezek 25 – 32), the bad news for the nations means good news for the houses of Jacob and Joseph.

2. The Ultimate Fate of Esau and the Nations (vv. 15b – 16)

After the opening theme statement, Obadiah's reversion to second person singular forms in v. 15b-c and his refocus of attention on Esau seem awkward,[12] but stylistic surprises like this are often the keys to the text and its rhetorical intent. Taking vv. 15b-c and 16 together, we discover that the implications of the prophet's invective against Esau extend for beyond the nation of Edom; Esau represents the nations, and his fate is paradigmatic of the fate that awaits them.

Obadiah begins his description of the day of YHWH with carefully constructed declarations of poetic justice (*talion*), consisting of two parts. The first, "As you have done, it shall be done to you" is rooted in Israel's legal tradition,[13] but the

prophets often apply it to nonlegal contexts.[14] Here Obadiah seems to have summarized what Ezekiel had spelled out in detail in his own oracle against Edom in 35:10 – 15:

[10]Because you have said, "These two nations and these two lands will belong to me, and we will possess them" — even though YHWH was there — [11]Therefore, by my life — the declaration of the Lord YHWH — *I will respond with the same anger and passion with which you in your hatred treated them.* I will make myself known through them when I punish you. [12]Then you will know that I am YHWH. I have heard all the taunts you shouted against the mountains of Israel: "It has been laid waste! They have been handed over to us to devour!" [13]With your arrogant speech[15] you have challenged me! With your boastful words you have defied me! I have heard [you] myself! [14]Thus has the Lord YHWH declared: While the whole world celebrates, I will make you a desolation. [15]*Just as you rejoiced over the possession of the house of Israel, because it was laid waste* [שָׁמֵמָה], *so I will deal with you:* You, Mount Seir, will become a wasteland [שְׁמָמָה], along with all Edom, the whole land. Then they will know that I am YHWH.[16]

The following clause reinforces the retributive nature of this administration of justice.[17] Indeed, the word order of v. 15d (SVM) focuses on the retribution.[18] Although the word גְּמוּל ("action") is often understood in terms of recompense or requital,[19] this sense derives more from the contexts in which the word occurs than the root (גמל)

---

11. Contra Raabe, *Obadiah*, 192.

12. Although many commentators and some translations (e.g., TNK), reverse v. 15a and v. 15b-c, to restore logic to the flow, as noted above, this undercuts the rhetorical force of the prophecy as a whole.

13. For the talionic principle in Israelite law, see Exod 21:23 – 25; Lev 24:19 – 20; Deut 19:18 – 21. However, Renkema (*Obadiah*, 188) rightly notes that this principle is not distinctly Israelite. Cf. the Law Code of Hammurabi, §§196 – 200.

14. 1 Sam 15:33; Jer 5:19; 50:15, 29; Ezek 16:59; Zech 7:13.

15. Literally, "you have made great against me with your mouth"; cf. Obadiah 12.

16. As translated by Block, *Ezekiel Chapters 25 – 48*, 312 – 24. Cf. also Ezek. 25:12 – 14.

17. Note the verb, אֶשְׁפֹּט, "I will judge," i.e., "I will execute the sentence," at the end of Ezek 35:11.

18. S = subject; V = verb; M = modifier. The normal/canonical order has the verb first.

19. E.g., *HALOT*, 196.

itself, which apparently means "to demonstrate, to treat someone" a certain way.[20] The action may involve either deeds of kindness[21] or evil deeds.[22] Here it obviously involves the latter, alluding to the catalogue of Esau's crimes against his brother in vv. 11 – 14. The following phrase, יָשׁוּב בְּרֹאשֶׁךָ, "your action shall return on your own head," involves a standard expression for retribution.[23] For a deed to return on one's head means that the actions the person has committed against or for the benefit of someone else, as well as their consequences, will come back on them; the subject will become the object. As Esau has done to others, so others will do to him. With poetic justice, the evils he has perpetrated against his brother Jacob will now be perpetrated against him.[24]

But who will execute this retributive justice? In v. 15c Esau's deeds appear as the subject of the verb, suggesting that the actions themselves will come back to haunt him. But this is obviously a figure of speech. While the passive verb (יֵעָשֶׂה, "it shall be done to you") leaves the agent of Esau's judgment unspecified, the opening lines in this book (v. 1c-f) had called on the nations to rise up against Edom. Indeed, although Obadiah's tone is less vindictive than that of the psalmist in Ps 137, and although the psalmist pleads for justice to be dealt to Babylon rather than Edom (137:7), Obadiah's assertion recalls 137:8: "O daughter Babylon, you devastator! How privileged will be the one who pays you

back the treatment with which you treated us" (אַשְׁרֵי שֶׁיְשַׁלֶּם לָךְ אֶת גְּמוּלֵךְ שֶׁגָּמַלְתְּ לָנוּ). Presumably the psalmist has some earthly power in mind.

However, since this is the day of YHWH, and since Ezekiel's oracles against this nation expressly portray YHWH as the executor of the judgment, ultimate responsibility for Esau's demise lies with him. He is the guarantor of the moral order and the righteous judge; he will ensure that justice is always served and evil always repaid. As Jeremiah affirms, "YHWH is a God who keeps account of human actions;[25] he will repay in full" (אֵל גְּמֻלוֹת יהוה שַׁלֵּם יְשַׁלֵּם; Jer 51:56).

In v. 16 Obadiah's attention shifts from retributive to distributive justice, promising that the tables will turn and ultimately the fate of Judah in 586 BC will be shared by all the nations. This statement consists of a protasis, setting up a comparison (v. 16a), followed by a quadruple apodosis describing the fate of the nations (v. 16b-e). Returning to the more general theme of YHWH's day against all the nations, Obadiah declares that all the strangers and foreigners who entered the gates of Jerusalem, carried off Jacob's nobility, and cast lots for the city (v. 11b-d) will drink the fury of YHWH's wrath.

The prophet keeps his hearers'/readers' focus on drinking by repeating the verb "to drink" (שָׁתָה, v. 16a, b, c). The association of divine fury with drinking has a long history in Israel, having been first introduced by YHWH himself in what

---

20. *HALOT*, 197. In Ps 103:10 the word is paired with עָשָׂה, "to do, to act."

21. 1 Sam 24:18[17]; Ps 116:7; Prov 31:12. Indeed by itself the word often means "to treat well" (2 Sam 19:37[36]; 22:21; Isa 63:7; Pss 13:6[5]; 18:21[20]; 119:17; 142:8[7]; Prov 11:17), which recalls the Akkadian cognate *gamālu*, "to perform a kind act" (*CAD* 5.21 – 22).

22. Gen 50:15, 17; Deut 32:6; 1 Sam 24:18[17]; Pss 7:5[4]; 137:8; Prov 3:30; Isa 3:9.

23. Num 5:7; Judg 9:57; 1 Sam 25:39; 1 Kgs 2:33, 44; Neh 3:36[4:4]; Ps 7:17[16]; Joel 4:4, 7[3:4, 7] (cf. הֵשִׁיב עַל רֹאשׁ, "to return on [one's] head" (Esth 9:25). Note also the idiom, "to put

on [one's] conduct on [one's] head" (נָתַן דֶּרֶךְ בְּרֹאשׁ: 1 Kgs 8:32; Ezek 9:10; 11:21; 16:43; 22:31.

24. Elsewhere such retribution is expressed with the verb שָׁלֵם, "to pay back" (e.g., Jer. 50:29). For additional references, see *HALOT*, 1534 – 35. This verb is often associated with גְּמוּל, "action, treatment": Isa 59:18b; 66:6; Jer 51:6; Joel 4:4[3:4]; Ps 137:8; Prov 19:17.

25. Although usually translated something like "God of requital" (e.g., Lundbom, *Jeremiah 37 – 52*, 495), the sense of "requital, compensation" derives from the context rather than the word itself. אֵל גְּמֻלוֹת seems to mean something like "the God who keeps account of human actions."

we may identify as Israel's national anthem (Deut 32).[26] Having described with vivid poetic imagery Israel's apparently inevitable apostasy, which will lead to her judgment at the hands of the nations, the song Moses taught his people predicts the ultimate demise of those nations whom YHWH had used to punish his people. Mixing his metaphors he declared their certain end:

> Their vine comes from the vinestock of Sodom,
>> from the vineyards of Gomorrah;
> their grapes are grapes of poison,
>> their clusters are bitter;
> their wine is the poison of serpents,
>> the cruel venom of asps.
>> (Deut 32:32 – 33, NRSV)

The notion of drinking wine (presumably poisoned) to the dregs as a metaphor for YHWH's certain judgment appears frequently in the prophets.[27] Although Ezek 23:32 – 34 offers the fullest description of the motif, Obadiah seems to have been inspired by Jeremiah. In Jer 25:17, 21 this prophet envisions receiving the cup from YHWH's hand and giving it to the nations — including Edom — to drink. But in the midst of the oracle against Edom, YHWH declares: "If those who do not deserve to drink the cup still have to drink it, shall you be the one to go unpunished? You shall not go unpunished; you must drink it" (Jer 41:12, NRSV). Obadiah does not specify what is drunk (wine? poison? the fury of YHWH?), but "you must drink" serves as a shorthand expression for consuming the wrath of YHWH.

But who is the subject of the verb "you (pl.) drank" (שְׁתִיתֶם), and what is the significance of the drinking in v. 16a? Several interpretations have been offered. First, some see here a reference to Esau's celebrating the defeat of Judah in 586 BC with revelry and drinking on YHWH's holy mountain.[28] This interpretation assumes that the second person references in v. 15b-c carry over into v. 16a. However, this interpretation suffers from three weaknesses: (1) it fails to take into account the discourse significance of the change from second person singular verbs in v. 15b-c to the plural form in v. 16a; (2) the OT never refers expressly to "drinking bouts" in celebration of victory;[29] (3) it requires a shift in the significance of the drinking, from Edom's celebration of victory in v. 16a to the nations' drinking divine judgment in v. 16b-d.

Others see the Edomites as the subject but understand their drinking as a future event, referring to Edom's inevitable demise along with the nations and her punishment for the crimes against Jacob.[30] This interpretation sees continuity between the second person verbs of v. 15b-c and v. 16a-d, both assuming Esau/Edom as the addressee. Accordingly, together v. 11b-e and v. 16a exhibit an impressive a b b′ a′ comparative structure:

a The nations have invaded and destroyed Jerusalem (v. 11b-d)
> b Esau acted just like the nations (v. 11e)
> b′ Esau will drink the fury of divine wrath (v. 16a)
a′ The nations will experience the same fate as Esau (v. 16b-d)

---

26. On which see Daniel I. Block, *Deuteronomy* (NIVAC; Grand Rapids: Zondervan, 2011), 746 – 49; idem, *How I Love Your Torah, O LORD! Studies in the Book of Deuteronomy* (Eugene, OR: Cascade, 2011), 162 – 84.

27. Isa 51:17, 22; Jer 49:12; 51:7; Ezek 23:32 – 34; Nah 3:11; Hab 2:16; cf. Ps 75:9[8]. For a thorough study of the metaphor of drinking the cup of divine wrath, see Raabe, *Obadiah*, 205 – 42.

28. Cf. the reference to the clamor raised in the house of YHWH as on a festival day in Lam. 2:7. Cf. Stuart, *Hosea-Jonah*, 420; Niehaus, "Obadiah," 535 – 36.

29. The closest we get is the bizarre feast involving animals eating human bodies and drinking their blood as table fare in Ezek 39:17 – 20. However, those who drink the blood of Gog and his hosts are not the victors, but invited guests.

30. Wendland, "Obadiah's 'Day,'" 37; Renkema, *Obadiah*, 191 – 95.

However, this interpretation is difficult to recon-
cile with the following phrase, "on my holy mountain," unless the scene of the crime becomes the
scene of the judgment, though this seems forced.[31]
Furthermore, it fails to account adequately for the
shift from second person singular forms in v. 15b-c
to the plural form of v. 16a, and it requires an awkward reading of the perfect verb, which usually
— though not always — denotes past completed
action.

While both interpretations are possible, it seems
best to assume that in v. 16a Obadiah addresses
his real audience, Judean and Israelite survivors
of the devastation of 586 BC.[32] The shift in addressee from v. 15b-c is signaled by the switch to
a plural verb שְׁתִיתֶם, "you drank" (Esau has con-
sistently been treated as singular) and reinforced
by references to Esau in the third person in v. 18c
and f and the insertion of a second focus particle,
"Indeed, surely" (כִּי; cf. v. 15a) at the beginning of
v. 16a, which alerts the hearer/reader to pay careful
attention to what follows. Accordingly, we should
treat the perfect verb שְׁתִיתֶם as a simple past, "you
drank," or a past perfect, "you have drunk." At the
same time the focus particle and the word order
fix attention on the action, that is, the drinking — a
focus that is retained in v. 16b-c.

Obadiah does not specify what Judah drank, but
he does note the location: "on my holy mountain."[33]
The expression "my holy mountain" is a favorite
expression in Isaiah,[34] but it also occurs in Ps 2:6
and Joel 4:17[3:17].[35] Usually the expression refers

either to Jerusalem (Isa 66:20; Joel 4:17[3:17]), or,
more specifically, as in v. 17a below, to Mount Zion
(Joel 2:1; 4:17[3:17]). In both instances it represents the center of Judah or even the territory of
Israel (Exod 15:17).

Obadiah's statement is remarkable on two
counts. First, YHWH claims it as *his* mountain. In
v. 13a YHWH had spoken of Jacob as "my people,"
despite having abandoned them and poured out
his fury on them. Now he speaks similarly of the
place where he had resided until 586 BC. Despite
his abandonment of the temple and his invitation
to Nebuchadnezzar's forces to destroy it (Ezek
8 – 11; cf. Ps 78:59 – 64), he had not forgotten his
irrevocable election of this site as his dwelling place
(Ps 132:13 – 15). Second, he refers to his mountain
as "holy," that is, set apart as his residence and
dedicated to his service.[36] This marks a radical
shift in the divine disposition, since the Judeans
had defiled it with their idolatrous abominations
(Ezek 8:1 – 18), and the nations had defiled it further by invading it and laying Jerusalem in ruins
(Ps 74:2 – 7; 79:1; Ezek 25:3; Mic 4:11). Indeed,
Obadiah seems to assume the fulfillment of Joel
4:17[3:17]:

> Then you will know that I am YHWH your God,
> who dwells in Zion, my holy mountain.

> And Jerusalem will be holy, and strangers [זָרִים]
> will never pass through it again.

Following v. 15b-c, Obadiah's prediction that
the nations, rather than Esau, would drink of the
cup of divine fury as Judah had is surprising, not

---

31. As does Renkema's explanation.

32. This is the natural reading if one transposes v. 15b-c to
the end of v. 14, as most critical scholars do. Cf. Barton, *Joel
and Obadiah*, 150 – 51.

33. The expression, עַל הַר קָדְשִׁי occurs elsewhere only in Isa
66:20, which speaks of some from among the nations bringing
the exiles of Israel/Judah to "my holy mountain Jerusalem," as
offerings to YHWH.

34. Six times: Isa 11:9; 56:7; 57:13; 65:11, 25; 66:20.

35. Note also "his holy mountain," Ps 48:21. ; 99:9.

36. On "holiness" as "set apart for divine service," see
Claude-Bernard Costecalde and P. Grelot, "Sacré (et sainteté),"
Supplément au Dictionnaire de la Bible, vol. 10 (Paris, 1985),
col. 1342 – 1483, particularly col. 1356 – 93; idem, *Aux origines
du sacre biblique* (Paris: Letouzey & Ane, 1986).

only in the light of the earlier focus on him in this book, but also in the light of Ps 137:7 and Lam 4:21:

> Rejoice and be glad, O daughter Edom,
>> you that live in the land of Uz;
> but to you also the cup shall pass;
>> you shall become drunk and strip yourself bare. (NRSV)

Instead Obadiah predicts the doom of the nations under the fury of YHWH. This changes the role of the nations from v. 1c-f, where they were commissioned by YHWH to punish Edom. Apparently Esau/Edom now serves a paradigmatic role, representing all the nations that had participated in Judah's/Jerusalem's demise. Obadiah intensifies their demise by adding תָּמִיד, which usually means "constantly" and is often translated this way here.[37] However, the following lines suggest that the issue here is not continuity, i.e., relentless drinking, as if this is a bottomless vessel. If the nations themselves cease to exist (v. 16e), surely their drinking must stop. Rather, the issue seems to be deep drinking; they will not stop until the cup is empty ("to the full").[38] The word functions as shorthand for "draining the cup to the dregs."[39]

This interpretation is reinforced by v. 16c-e as the prophet describes the effects of the nations' drinking. After reiterating that "they shall drink," he adds a verb that is difficult to interpret because it is so rare. Most translations assume וְלָעוּ involves a hapax verb (l‘‘) from the same semantic field as שָׁתָה, "to drink."[40] However, the word seems to involve another homonymous Hebrew root denoting incoherent or rash speech (Job 6:3; Prov 20:25), in which case the reference is to the effects of drinking on the imbibers' speech.[41] Accordingly, the word functions as shorthand for this and other evidences of intoxication. Specific effects of too much wine mentioned elsewhere include being drunk,[42] vomiting[43] or wallowing in vomit,[44] being out of one's mind/acting like a mad man,[45] falling over,[46] and staggering with intoxication.[47]

Obadiah ends this brief treatment of the nations' drinking the cup of divine wrath in v. 16e with a declaration of their ultimate removal from the scene. The statement, "And they shall be as if they had never existed" (וְהָיוּ כְּלוֹא הָיוּ), does not declare the end of their existence; rather, it summarizes their loss of significance in the grand divine scheme of history.[48] In a dramatic reversal, once their task of dealing with Edom is over (v. 1c-f), they will become like Edom herself: small and insignificant (v. 2). This may be bad news for Esau and the nations, but it is extremely good news for Jacob, for it means that nothing will stop YHWH from fulfilling the plan for him that he set in place long ago.

---

37. Thus NIV. Based on several minor manuscripts, some emend תָּמִיד to סָבִיב, "around you." Thus NRSV; Barton, *Joel and Obadiah*, 151; Raabe, *Obadiah*, 204–5.

38. Cf. Renkema, *Obadiah*, 195–96, who unnecessarily emends תָּמִיד to תמים, "perfect, complete."

39. Elsewhere this notion is expressed more explicitly in several forms. Ps 75:8[7], "They will drain its sherds/dregs, they will drink" (שְׁמָרֶיהָ יִמְצוּ יִשְׁתּוּ); Ezek 23:34, "And they will drink it and drain [it], and gnaw its sherds/dregs" (וְשָׁתִית אוֹתָהּ וּמָצִית וְאֶת־חֲרָשֶׂיהָ תְּגָרֵמִי).

40. "To swallow" (NASB, ESV); "they will drink and drink" (NIV); "to gulp down (NRSV); cf. "to slurp," *HALOT*, 533.

41. Cf. TNK, "drink till their speech grows thick"; Renkema (*Obadiah*, 197), "drunken talk."

42. Heb שָׁכַר, Jer 25:27.

43. Heb הִתְגֹּעֲשׁוּ, Jer 25:16; cf. LXX, ἐξεμοῦνται, "to vomit, disgorge." See *HALOT*, 200. Also Heb קִיא/קָאָה, Jer 25:27.

44. Heb סָפַק בְּקִיאוֹ, Jer 48:26.

45. Jer. 25:16. Heb הִתְהֹלֵל: 1 Sam 21:14; Jer 50:38; 51:7.

46. Heb נָפַל, Jer 25:27.

47. Heb תַּרְעֵלָה, Isa 51:17, 22; Ps 60:5[3]).

48. On כְּלוֹא, "like not," meaning "as if not," see JM §174d.

3. The Contrasting Fate of Jacob (vv. 17 – 18)

The marked construction of v. 17a ("But on Mount Zion")[49] signals a shift in focus, from the nations drunk and debased by the fury of YHWH's wrath, to his holy mountain (v. 16a), where order reigns, and the tripartite covenant involving YHWH, the house of Jacob, and the land is fully operative. The calamities of 598 and 586 BC had left what remained of the Israelites angry and deeply disillusioned. In their minds YHWH had reneged on all his promises. In the hour of deepest need he had abandoned his temple, his eternal dwelling place (Ps 132:13 – 18), and the symbol of Israel's security (Jer 7:1 – 7); he had abandoned his people, breaking his commitment to Abraham and ratified with his descendants at Sinai, to be their God forever,[50] and he had allowed the Babylonians to expel them from the land promised them as their eternal possession (Gen 17:8). If the demise of Esau and the nations promised in vv. 15 – 16 hinted at a new day for Israel, in vv. 17 – 18 that hope is concretized.

Obadiah's expression of that hope has two dimensions. First, the hope of Jacob rests in the full restoration of covenantal relationships; that is, Mount Zion will be restored as the residence of YHWH and Israel will be restored to her land (v. 17). Apart from the marked syntax of v. 17a-b, the meaning of both lines is unclear. Most translations render the first line something like, "But on Mount Zion there shall be those that escape"

(NRSV), as if פְּלֵיטָה functions as a collective for "escapees," equivalent to פְּלִיטִים, "escapees/fugitives," in v. 14a. However, the shift from a concrete masculine plural noun to an abstract feminine noun seems intentional. The present form may indeed be used concretely of those who have escaped, but usually in these contexts it will be definite or qualified.[51] As in other contexts involving the day of YHWH, especially when combined with the verb הָיָה, "to be," the unqualified word refers to the escape from battle itself (not escapees).[52]

The link between our text and Joel 3:5[2:32] is especially striking:

Joel 3:5[2:32]:
    For on Mount Zion and in Jerusalem
    there shall be an escape.

Obadiah 17a:
    For on Mount Zion
    there shall be an escape.[53]

In both instances "escape" is actually the subject of the verb: literally, "On Mount Zion escape will be." Coming immediately after vv. 15 – 16, on first sight Obadiah seems to envision Mount Zion as a refuge for those among the nations experiencing the awful day of YHWH. However, it is clear from v. 17c that the refuge is for the benefit of the house of Jacob, presenting the starkest contrast to the scene described in vv. 11 – 14, where on "the day of Jacob" Jerusalem offered no refuge at all from the heat of the divine wrath. Furthermore, Jacob's

---

49. Following this opening adverbial phrase, vv. 17 – 18 are held together by the sequence of verbs: imperfect (תִּהְיֶה) + waw consecutive perfect (וְהָיָה) + waw consecutive perfect (וְיָרְשׁוּ) + waw consecutive perfect (וְהָיָה) + waw consecutive perfect (וְדָלְקוּ) + waw consecutive perfect (וַאֲכָלוּם).

50. Gen 17:7; Exod 31:16 – 17; Lev 24:8; Judg 2:1; Ps 11:2 – 9; Isa 24:4 – 5; 54:4 – 10; Jer 31:35 – 37.

51. Judg 21:17 (Benjaminites); 2 Kgs 19:30 – 31 = Isa 37:31 – 32 (Judeans); Ezra 9:8, 13 – 15; Neh. 1:2 (post-exilic

community); 1 Chr 4:43 (Amalekites); 2 Chr 30:6 (Israelites); Isa 4:2; 10:20 (Israel); 15:9 (Moab); Ezek 14:22 (inhabitants of Jerusalem). In Exod 10:5 it refers to agricultural products that survive a hailstorm. In 2 Kgs 19:31 = Isa. 37:32, פְּלֵיטָה is conjoined with שְׁאֵרִית, "remnant," that goes out from Mount Zion.

52. Jer 50:29; Joel 2:3; 3:5[2:32]; also Gen 45:7; 2 Sam 15:14; cf. 2 Chr 20:24 ("There was no escape," a verbless clause).

53. Joel 3:5[2:32]: וּבִירוּשָׁלַ͏ִם תִּהְיֶה פְלֵיטָה   כִּי בְהַר־צִיּוֹן.
    Obadiah 17a: תִּהְיֶה פְלֵיטָה   וּבְהַר צִיּוֹן.

brother had aided and abetted the disaster by cutting off and handing over to enemies those who tried to escape. Now Obadiah anticipates a complete turnaround in fortunes, and, though using different vocabulary, the realization of the hope promised in Isa 14:32 ("YHWH has founded Zion, and the needy among his people will take refuge [חָסָה] in her") and in Joel 4:16[3:16] ("YHWH may roar from Zion, and bellow out from Jerusalem; the heavens and the earth may shake, but YHWH will be a refuge [מַחֲסֶה] for his people, a stronghold [מָעוֹז] for the people of Israel").

But there is more to the transformation of Zion: holiness will pervade the city that had been profaned by Israel's abominations, desecrated by the presence of foreigners and strangers, and polvluted by the blood of the slain. Again, although most translations treat Zion as the subject of the verb וְהָיָה, as in Joel 4:17[3:17], here "holiness" (קֹדֶשׁ) is actually the subject. This interpretation is confirmed by a comparison of the syntax of these two texts:

Joel 4:17[3:17]:
    And Jerusalem will be holy.
    וְהָיְתָה יְרוּשָׁלַ͏ִם קֹדֶשׁ

Obadiah 17b:
    And there shall be holiness.
    וְהָיָה קֹדֶשׁ

Whereas the feminine verb in the Joel text applies the holiness specifically to the place, Jerusalem, Obadiah declares that on the future day of YHWH holiness will pervade Zion. When the nations will be utterly humiliated under the furious hand of God and when their territories apparently will be desecrated, YHWH will respond to the la-

ments of his people, and his mountain will be sanctified once more (cf. v. 16a).

The prophet does not explain how Jerusalem will be transformed. Although Ezekiel prophesied far away in Babylon, the links between his oracles against Edom and Obadiah's own prophecies suggest the latter was familiar with the former's work. Indeed this statement summarizes with two short words what had taken Ezekiel nine chapters to describe (Ezek 40 – 48). In his final vision Ezekiel foresaw a day when the temple would be rebuilt with massive walls and gates on a high mountain, when YHWH would once more take up residence on his throne and dwell among his people forever, when the place itself would embody supreme holiness (43:1 – 12),[54] when worshipers and the worship itself would be holy, when the river that flowed from the mountain would rejuvenate the landscape (47:1 – 12), and when the land itself would be holy (47:1 – 48:35). The name of the city says it all: יהוה שָׁמָּה, "YHWH is there."

Joel had likewise summarized the message of Ezek 40 – 48 with a single statement: "Then you will know that I am YHWH your God, who dwells in Zion, my holy mountain. And Jerusalem shall be holy, and strangers shall never again pass through it" (Joel 4:17[3:17]). Like Mount Sinai itself centuries earlier (Exod 3:5), this place will be transformed by the presence of God. Neither the people nor the sanctity of the place will again be threatened by strangers.

However, the transformation is not restricted to Mount Zion. In v. 17c Obadiah declares that Israel's relationship to its patrimonial territory will also be restored. The prophet continues to highlight the familial context by referring to the beneficiaries of

---

54. Hebrew קֹדֶשׁ קָדָשִׁים in Ezek 43:12 denotes "extreme/perfect holiness."

the restoration as "the house of Jacob" (בֵּית יַעֲקֹב). This expression links this statement to v. 10b, where Obadiah had referred to the patronymic ancestor (Jacob) as Esau's brother, but it also highlights the perception of Israel as an ethnic group, a large extended family descended from a single ancestor from whom they derive their name,[55] corresponding to the Edomites, who represent "the house of Esau" (בֵּית עֵשָׂו, v. 18c). Since Obadiah will juxtapose "house of Jacob" and "house of Joseph" in v. 18a-b, here Jacob represents Judah, that is, what was left of Israel after the northern kingdom was defeated and its population scattered throughout the Assyrian empire in the aftermath of the fall of Samaria in 722 BC.

Obadiah identifies the benefaction the house of Jacob will enjoy as "possess[ing] their own possessions" (וְיָרְשׁוּ אֵת מוֹרָשֵׁיהֶם). The root ירשׁ, "to possess, claim," occurs 230 times in the OT, usually with reference to land as the object.[56] The expression is especially common in Deuteronomy, where the root occurs more than 70 times, generally relating to the Promised Land as the territory that YHWH gives to them and invites them to "possess" (e.g., Deut 1:8) by "dispossessing" the Canaanites.[57] While in Deuteronomy the common noun "possession," derived from this root, is יְרֻשָּׁה,[58] Ezekiel prefers מוֹרָשָׁה.[59] Obadiah's מוֹרָשׁ occurs elsewhere only in Isa 14:23. This vocabulary links Jacob's

future with his past. The land that YHWH had delivered into Israel's hands in fulfillment of his promises (Gen 15:7 – 8), but which they had lost when enemies invaded it and deported the significant part of population (Obad 11b-d), would be returned to them.

The relationship between v. 17c and v. 18a-e is that of topic and exposition; the latter explains how the former will transpire. Here Obadiah borrows an image that was common in ancient battle scenes.[60] Adopting a scorched-earth policy, invaders would torch the cities they conquered as well as the surrounding fields and orchards, thereby depriving the victims of necessary resources for life. Indeed, in the original conquest of Canaan, YHWH, the divine warrior, who went before Israel identified himself as "Consuming Fire."[61] However, here YHWH places the torch in the hands of the houses of Jacob and Joseph and sends them out to burn the house of Esau like straw.

The noun קַשׁ, which may denote chaff, straw, or stubble, refers to the dried remains of grain after the kernels have been removed. This material is extremely combustible, which makes it an apt metaphor for judgment.[62] Although v. 18a-c is governed by a single verb verb "to be" (וְהָיָה), the relationship between a and b on the one hand and c on the other is asymmetrical. The houses of Jacob and Joseph are "fire" and "flame" respectively, but the house

---

55. For a full discussion of this form of national name, see Daniel I. Block, "Israel's House: Reflections on the Use of בית ישראל in the Old Testament in the Light of Its Ancient Near Eastern Environment," *JETS* 28 (1985): 257 – 75.

56. Often in association with נַחֲלָה, "special grant" (e.g., Num 27:11), or אֲחֻזָּה, "possession" (e.g., Lev 25:46).

57. When people are the object, the verb ירשׁ means "to dispossess, expel." See Deut 9:1, 5; 12:2, 29; 18:14; 19:1.

58. Deut 2:5, 9, 12, 19; 3:20.

59. Seven of the nine occurrences are found in Ezekiel: Ezek. 11:15; 25:4, 10; 33:24; 36:2, 3, 5; it occurs elsewhere only in Exod. 6:8 and Deut. 33:4 (poetic).

60. See the Lachish reliefs of Sennacherib, in *ANEP*, ##371 – 74, pp. 129 – 32.

61. The syntax of Deut 4:24 and 9:3 suggests אֵשׁ אֹכְלָה is an epithet of deity, not merely an adjective. Deut. 29:23 anticipates YHWH burning his own land like he had previously burned up Sodom and Gomorrah. On these texts, see Block, *Deuteronomy*, 684 – 85.

62. Exod 15:7; Isa 5:24; 47:14; Joel 2:5; Nah 1:10; Mal 3:19. The terms "flame" (לֶהָבָה) and "fire" (אֵשׁ) are often paired: Num 21:28; Pss 83:15[14]; 106:18; Isa 5:24; 10:17; 43:2; 47:14; Jer 48:45; Joel 1:19, 23. Cf. also Pss 29:7; 105:32; Isa 4:5; Hos 7:6; Lam 2:3.

of Esau will become straw.[63] Esau may appear to be strong now, but he is about to be transformed.

In v. 18a-c Obadiah identifies and characterizes the principals in this application of the metaphor. As noted earlier, the protagonists are the house of Jacob and the house of Joseph, here obviously referring to what is left of the kingdom of Judah and the northern kingdom of Israel, respectively. Neither the rest of the prophets nor any other text in the OT employs this combination of names. While historiographic texts tend to identify them as the houses/people of Judah and Israel respectively, the prophets speak of Judah and Ephraim,[64] or of Judah and Joseph;[65] for Obadiah to speak of "Jacob" and "Joseph" is remarkable on several counts. First, "Jacob" was the ancestor to all the tribes, but here the roles are reversed. Whereas elsewhere "Israel" identifies the northern kingdom because it consisted of the majority of tribes, in contrast to "Judah," which identified a single tribe, here the name of the ancestor of all the tribes ("Jacob") is identified with a single tribe (Judah).

Second, whereas to this point Obadiah's words have been directed to the survivors of the fall of Judah, who alone would have been affected by the encroachment of Edom, he casts his vision beyond Judah to the northern tribes, which had disappeared from history in the eighth century.

Third, as in the cases where Joseph represents the northern kingdom, the name reflects awareness not only of the history of the northern kingdom, in which the tribe of Ephraim was the dominant political power from the beginning, but also the traditions of tribal origins, according to which Ephraim — rather than Manasseh — was the designated "firstborn" of Joseph (Gen 48:1 – 22; cf. 49:22 – 26; Deut 33:13 – 17).

By inserting the northern kingdom into his vision of Israel's restoration, Obadiah follows his predecessors Hosea (Hos 2:2) and Ezekiel (Ezek 37:15 – 17). The vision of all Israel restored to the land derives not only from the memory of the twelve tribes' common origin in Jacob/Israel, their common participation in the exodus, and their common reception of the land of Canaan as their divinely allotted territory, but also in the memory of their membership in the old kingdom of David (cf. 2 Sam. 5:1 – 5). Indeed, in Ezekiel's vision of Israel's future, over his flock YHWH will appoint one shepherd, his servant David (Ezek 34:23 – 24), and he will reunite the separate kingdoms into a single political entity (גּוֹי אֶחָד) in the land on the mountains of Israel, with a single king over them all, ending the schism involving two "nations" (גּוֹיִם) and two "kingdoms" (מַמְלָכוֹת, 37:21 – 22). Obadiah's remarkable statement affirms that YHWH has not forgotten his ancient promises to all Israel, nor has he stifled forever his compassion toward any portion thereof.

Verse 18d-f summarizes the divine mandate for the houses of Jacob and Joseph: burn and consume the house of Esau, leaving no survivor (שָׂרִיד).[66] Obadiah's audience would no doubt have grasped the ambiguity of the expression "house of Esau" at this point. While it seems Obadiah coined the phrase as a counterpart to the houses of Jacob and Joseph in order to refer to the Edomites as a collective (hence the plural suffixes in v. 18d-e), the reference to "house" also evokes a more concrete image: the sight of Edom's houses going up in flames. According to v. 18f, when people sift

---

63. The construction, הָיָה + לְ means "to become, to turn into."

64. Isa 7:17; 11:13 – 14; Hos 5:5, 12 – 14; 6:5; 11:12; Zech 9:13.

65. Ezek 37:16, 19, though here Joseph is clarified as "Ephraim."

66. On this word, see above on v. 14c.

through the rubble in the aftermath of the fire, they will find no survivors. Although the point will be developed further in vv. 19a and 21b, the present statement suggests that Judah and Joseph are free to take over the land. Obadiah seems hereby to build on Ezekiel, who had declared explicitly that YHWH has authorized Israel to execute vengeance on his behalf against Edom (Ezek 25:14).[67] However, Balaam seems to have anticipated this many centuries earlier:

> Edom will become a possession [יְרֵשָׁה],
> > Seir a possession of its enemies,
> > while Israel does valiantly.
> One out of Jacob shall rule,
> > and destroy the survivors [שָׂרִיד] of Ir.
> > > > (Num 24:18 – 19 NRSV)[68]

But we should not push the issue too far. If Israel becomes the agent of divine fury against the enemy, the goal is not so much the occupation of enemy territory as the full elimination of outside threats, so that 586 BC never happens again.

Instead of stamping this paragraph with the signatory formula (cf. vv. 4d, 8b), the prophet concludes with the divine declaration formula, "for YHWH has spoken" (כִּי יהוה דִּבֵּר). Compared to other prophetic formulas, this one is rare.[69] In most instances it appears at the conclusion of an utterance. Here it reinforces the notion that Obadiah's vision of a restored future is not a private dream of better days to come. Those who reject his message have in fact rejected YHWH, who stands behind the prophet's words as the divine Guarantor.

---

67. So also Renkema, *Obadiah*, 204.

68. Echoes of this text may be heard in Obadiah's vocabulary of possession (ירשׁ), survivors (שָׂרִיד), and doing valiantly (חַיִל, cf. v. 11b).

69. The simple form of the formula occurs nine times: Num 10:29; 1 Kgs 14:11; Isa 1:2; 22:25; 24:3; 25:8; Jer 13:15; Joel 4:8[3:8] Obad 18. Variations occur in Isa 1:20; 21:17; 24:3; 40:5; 58:14; Mic 4:4.

Obadiah 19 – 21

E. The Good Good News:
The Restoration of Jacob on the "Day of YHWH"

Main Idea of the Passage

The sure word of YHWH guarantees both Israel's full restoration to and occupation of the land promised them by his irrevocable covenant centuries ago and YHWH's ultimate rule over all.

Literary Context

The *waw* consecutive perfects (וְקָטַל forms) continue throughout this section, which suggests that despite the declaration formula in v. 18g, these sections should be read in tandem. Nevertheless the references to Mount Esau in vv. 19a and 21a create an effective inclusio. Remarkably the material between these references to Esau has little to do with Jacob's brother. Instead the attention is distributed among different elements of greater Israel and different regions of the land of Canaan. This section and the book as a whole reach a dramatic conclusion with the final declaration of YHWH's rule over all.

Translation and Exegetical Outline

Obadiah 19–21

	Hebrew	Translation
19a	וְיָרְשׁוּ הַנֶּגֶב אֶת־הַר עֵשָׂו	And the Negev will possess Mount Esau,
19b	וְהַשְּׁפֵלָה אֶת־פְּלִשְׁתִּים	and the Shephelah [will dispossess] the Philistines.
19c	וְיָרְשׁוּ אֶת־שְׂדֵה אֶפְרַיִם	And [. . . .] will possess the mountain of Ephraim*
19d	וְאֵת שְׂדֵה שֹׁמְרוֹן	and the field of Samaria,
19e	וּבִנְיָמִן אֶת־הַגִּלְעָד׃	and Benjamin [will possess] Gilead.
20a	וְגָלֻת הַחֵל־הַזֶּה	And as for the exiles of Halah†
20b	לִבְנֵי יִשְׂרָאֵל	belonging to the people of Israel,
20c	אֲשֶׁר־כְּנַעֲנִים עַד־צָרְפַת	[they will dispossess]‡ the Canaanites as far as Zarephath.
20d	וְגָלֻת יְרוּשָׁלִַם אֲשֶׁר בִּסְפָרַד	And as for the exiles of Jerusalem who are in Sepharad,
21a	יִרְשׁוּ אֵת עָרֵי הַנֶּגֶב׃	they will possess the towns of the Negev.
21b	וְעָלוּ מוֹשִׁעִים בְּהַר צִיּוֹן לִשְׁפֹּט אֶת־הַר עֵשָׂו	Saviors will go up to Mount Zion to rule Mount Esau,
21c	וְהָיְתָה לַיהוָה הַמְּלוּכָה׃	and the dominion will belong to YHWH.

E. The Good Good News: The Restoration of Jacob on the "Day of YHWH" (vv. 19–21)

1. The Restoration of Jacob's Land

2. The restoration of YHWH's Rule

---

*The text appears to be corrupt in two respects: (a) the subject of the verb has dropped out; (b) MT reads שְׂדֵה אֶפְרַיִם, "field of Ephraim," whereas LXX reads τὸ ὄρος Εφραιμ, "the mountain of Ephraim." Whereas "field of Ephraim" occurs nowhere else, "mountain/hill country of Ephraim" is common (Josh 17:15; Judg 7:24; 17:8; 18:2, 13; 19:1, 18; 2 Chr 19:4). The substitution of "field" for "mountain" looks like a dittographic error.

†Hebrew הַחֵל לַזֶּה is difficult. Some versions seemed to read לַחֵיל as a contraction for לַחַיִל, "company, host": cf. Targum, עַם, "people"; Vulgate, *exercitus*, "army." LXX ἡ ἀρχὴ αὕτη, "this domain," may have read לַחֹק, "allotment, portion." Our reading follows the suggestion of BHS.

‡Assuming אֲשֶׁר represents a corruption of an original יִירְשׁוּ, perhaps a dittographic error influenced by v. 20c. See commentary.

Structure and Literary Form

The formatting in *BHS* recognizes the shift in style in this last segment of Obadiah. Whereas vv. 1 – 18 have been formatted as poetry, these verses are formatted as continuous prose. We do not quarrel with the latter decision; the problem lies with the earlier. As acknowledged in the introduction, stylistic features of prose increase here, but this does not mean the preceding is poetry — unless the word has no meaning. The entire book is written in terse elevated prose, the style being chosen for maximum rhetorical effect. This segment subdivides into two uneven sections, the first describing the future restoration of Israel's land (vv. 19 – 20), and the second declaring Israel's supremacy over Esau and YHWH's supremacy over all (v. 21). The first divides further in two parts (vv. 19 and 20), the transition to the second being marked by the suspension of the verb as the defining factor and replaced by the noun גָּלוּת, "exile," which heightens the significance of this paragraph.[1]

The *Leitwort* (key word) of vv. 19 – 20 is obviously the waw consecutive perfect verb יָרַשׁ, "to possess," picked up from v. 17c and repeated three times (vv. 19a, c, 20d), and assumed at least three more times (vv. 19b, d, 20b). Apart from this verb, the paragraph is dominated by proper names, distributed among regional geographic names (Negev, Mount Esau, Shephelah, Gilead), names of specific towns (Samaria, Zarephath, Sepharad; cf. "towns of the Negeb" in v. 20d), Israelite tribal names (Ephraim, Benjamin), and gentilics (Philistines, Canaanites). Some of the constructions are awkward: (1) Negeb, a place name, is said to possess Mount Esau, which involves a personal name. (2) Shephelah, a place name, possesses the Philistines, a gentilic ethnic designation — we expect the reverse. (3) גָּלוּת, an abstract designation for "exile," occurs as the subject of the verb "to possess." (4) Structurally this section is framed by references to the Negev (the second word in v. 19a and the last word in v. 20d), but the name plays two different roles. In the first, it represents claimants to territory; in the second it represents the territory claimed. Stylistically and syntactically this paragraph is extremely rough and has the appearance of an unfinished first draft.[2]

---

1. Many isolate vv. 20 – 21 as a late, postexilic insertion.

2. For discussion of how critical scholars have treated the text, see Raabe, *Obadiah*, 256 – 58.

Explanation of the Text

1. The Restoration of Jacob's Land (vv. 19 – 20)

Verses 19 – 20 consist of three pairs of lines. In each pair one of the lines is especially problematic. In the first two pairs the major difficulties occur in the second line; in the third pair they occur in the first line. This pair of lines exhibits semantic elliptical parallelism in which the meaning of line A corresponds roughly to that of line B. As is common in parallelism, the verb is dropped from the second line but is implied from the first. The word order is canonical (i.e., verb + subject + object), with the focus being on the action of the subject possessing the object. However, each subject and each object requires comment.

The Negev (הַנֶּגֶב) refers to the region covering southern Judah and stretching into the Sinai peninsula. The term נֶגֶב means "dry ground" and was originally applied to the barren desert of southern Judah (Josh 15:2 – 4; 18:19; 1 Sam 27:10); it eventually referred more generally to the southland (Josh 11:2; 1 Sam 30:14; Zech 14:10), including the areas around Arad and Beersheba and southward. Since it was largely inhospitable, Judahite control over this region was often tenuous. Crossing the Arabah south of the Dead Sea, in the seventh to sixth centuries BC, Edomite encroachment on Judahite territory was naturally strongest in the Negev, which probably explains why Obadiah begins his geographic survey here. Since "the Negev" is a geographic term and never serves as the subject of

an active verb elsewhere, here the word is a metonymy for the people inhabiting the region. As in v. 8d Mount Esau refers generally to the mountainous heartland (Seir) of Edom, east of the Arabah, which means this statement reverses the direction of influence and control from that which obtained in Obadiah's day.

The second line involves several interesting details. First, like the Negev, "the Shephelah," the subject of an assumed verb, is also a geographic expression. The name means "lowland" and reflects the Judean perspective, looking from the Judean highlands toward the west. The Shephelah identified the foothills between the coastal plain and the central mountainous spine. Although assigned to Judah and Dan, this region frequently felt the pressure of the Philistines, who occupied the coastal plain and had competed for control of this region since premonarchic times (Judg 13 – 16).

The name פְּלִשְׁתִּים[3] derives from the name of one of a group of Sea Peoples who seem to have arrived in Canaan from the Aegean in two directions, some coming overland through Anatolia, the rest by sea via Crete[4] and Cyprus.[5] Those who entered Canaan by sea originally had their sights on Egypt. However, around 1190 BC they were defeated by Ramesses III, who engaged many of the defeated troops as mercenaries and stationed them in the coastal towns of Gaza, Ashkelon, and Ashdod.[6] Given the timing of the Philistines' arrival in Canaan, a clash with the Israelites, who had recently arrived from the east across the Jordan, was inevi-

---

3. Usually lacking the article, פְּלִשְׁתִּים, a gentilic, is considered a proper noun, hence the presence of the sign of the definite direct object (אֵת). The article occurs in a handful of texts: 1 Sam 4:7; 7:13; 13:20; 17:51 – 52; 2 Sam 5:19; 21:12; 2 Chr 21:16. In Egyptian writings Philistines are identified as *P-r-š-t-w*.

4. Caphtor in the Bible. Cf. Jer 47:4; Amos 9:7.

5. Kittim in the Bible. Cf. Num 24:24, where "ships will come from the shores of Cyprus [Kittim]" may refer to the first of several waves of new arrivals, generally referred to as the Sea Peoples.

6. Cf. Deut 2:23, which refers to Caphtorites. The Egyptian connection is also reflected in Gen 10:13 – 14.

table.[7] Although David seems to have eliminated the Philistines as serious contenders for control of the Shephelah, they were still around in the late seventh and early sixth centuries. Both Jeremiah (Jer 47:1–7) and Ezekiel (Ezek 25:15–17) predicted their doom. Although Ezekiel is vague on the Philistine participation in Judah's downfall, Joel is crystal clear:

> What are you to me, O Tyre and Sidon, and all
> the regions of Philistia?
> Are you paying me back for something?
> If you are paying me back,
> I will turn your deeds back upon your own heads
> swiftly and speedily.
> For you have taken my silver and my gold,
> and have carried my rich treasures into your temples.
> You have sold the people of Judah and Jerusalem
> to the Greeks,
> removing them far from their own border.
>
> (Joel 4:4–6[3:4–6])[8]

Now Obadiah joins this prophetic chorus,[9] anticipating the day when the inhabitants of the Shephelah will finally occupy the territory held for centuries by Philistines but promised originally to Israel.[10] Once again we note an irony in Obadiah's pronouncement: a territory (Shephelah) will dispossess[11] a people group (the Philistines). Normally it works in the opposite direction; people possess territory.

וְיָרְשׁוּ [...]	אֶת־שְׂדֵה אֶפְרַיִם
בִנְיָמִן [וְיָרַשׁ]	וְאֵת שְׂדֵה שֹׁמְרוֹן
	אֶת־הַגִּלְעָד
And [...] will possess	the field of Ephraim
	and the field of Samaria,
and Benjamin [will possess]	Gilead.

The interpretive problems increase in v. 19c-d. Although they are disproportionate in length, again we should construe these as a roughly parallel pair. In this section Obadiah's attention shifts from the south and west to the north and east of Judah, as representatives of Jacob and Joseph reclaim the territory of Ephraim and Gilead. We do not know whom the prophet has in mind as the subject of the verb in v. 19c, since apparently the subject has fallen out in the course of transmission.[12] As a double object, "the field of Ephraim" reflects the tribal territory dominated by the central ridge in the landscape of Ephraim, while "the field of Samaria" focuses attention on the area in and around the capital city.[13] Samaria was established as the capital city of the northern kingdom of Israel in the ninth century BC under the

---

7. The Samson cycle in Judg 13–16 reflects the tensions that existed between these two groups in the centuries leading up to the establishment of the monarchy in Israel. Although David served Achish the king of Philistine Gath as a vassal during his flight from Saul (1 Sam 27, 29), through a series of victories before (1 Sam 17–18) and after (2 Sam 5:17–25) his assumption of the kingship, the Philistine menace was resolved, though the Philistines did not go away. Cf. Isa 9:12.

8. NRSV text, formatted as poetry.

9. Cf. also Isa 14:29–32; Amos 1:8; Zeph 2:5; Zech 9:7.

10. Gen 15:18–21; 28:13–14; Exod 23:31; Num 34:6; Josh 1:4; 13:2–3. Joshua 15:33–47 includes the coastal towns under the heading of "Shephelah" (v. 33), suggesting biblical usage of this term was adjusted to political and geographic realities.

11. As noted above, when people are the objects of the verb יָרַשׁ the word means "to dispossess."

12. Renkema (*Obadiah*, 208–9) suggests Ephraim is the subject, but since Samaria is the capital of Ephraim, this interpretation has a subject reclaiming its own territory, which occurs nowhere else in this list. It is possible that "the Negev" and "the Shephelah" from v. 19a-b are assumed as the subject, but given the other textual difficulties and the supposed parallel with v. 19d, it is preferable to imagine the original subject has inadvertently been dropped.

13. Hebrew שָׂדֶה, "field," is used in three primary senses: (a) the habitat of wild animals, as opposed to מוֹשָׁב, land occupied by humans; (b) the land around a town, as opposed to עִיר, "town, city"; (c) fields where crops are grown, as opposed to בַּיִת, "house, home compound." For fuller discussion of the word, including its use as a designation for national territory, see Daniel I. Block, *The Foundations of National Identity: A Study in Ancient Near Northwest Semitic Perceptions* (Ann Arbor: UMI Dissertation Services, 1983), 327–39.

Omrides (1 Kgs 16:24), and it continued to function as such until its destruction by the Assyrians in 722 – 721 BC.[14] In keeping with the reference to the "house of Joseph" (v. 18b), this note reinforces the notion that the northern kingdom is fully integrated with Judah in Obadiah's vision for Israel's future. It also respects the historical significance of Samaria, which had for centuries competed with Jerusalem as a political center but had also been at the heart of northern apostasy (1 Kgs 16:29 – 33).

According to the tribal allotments in Josh 18:11 – 28, the territory of Benjamin was sandwiched between Judah and Ephraim. Here Obadiah envisions Benjamin crossing the Jordan and claiming the territory of Gilead. This name, which regularly appears with the article, הַגִּלְעָד, "the Gilead," refers to the hill country of the Transjordan, on both sides of the River Jabbok. Although the region was originally assigned to Reuben, Gad, and the half tribe of Manasseh (Deut 3:10 – 16; Josh 22:9), Benjamite links to this region across the river from their own land date to the premonarchic period. After the outrage at Gibeah and the civil war between the rest of the tribes and Benjamin, the latter was saved from extinction through a questionable legal move by which the Israelites authorized the surviving Benjamite troops to marry virgins from Jabesh-Gilead, who had themselves been spared in the massacre of the town's population

(Judg 21:8 – 12).[15] Later Saul, who was probably a descendant of one of these women, came to the defense of Jabesh-Gilead in the face of the threat from Bene Ammon (1 Sam 11:1 – 11). To express their gratitude, the people of Jabesh-Gilead buried the bones of Saul and his sons in Jabesh and mourned his death for seven days (1 Sam 31:11 – 13).

The four expansions in v. 19 reflect the four points of the compass: north (Ephraim), south (Mount Esau), East (Gilead), and West (the Philistines). While considerably more modest, Obadiah's references to places/nations representing the compass points follows a pattern found in Ezekiel's portrait of the worldwide alliance against Israel in the Gog oracle,[16] as well as Zephaniah's oracles of doom for the nations.[17] The latter is especially significant because it speaks expressly of the remnant of the house of Judah occupying enemy territory (Zeph 2:6 – 7).

Although v. 20 also involves a pair of roughly parallel lines, the textual problems in this verse exceed those of v. 19c-d.[18] We may make sense of this verse by reformatting the text in the table on p. 103.

This reading assumes the verb יְרְשׁוּ, "they will possess," and the direct object marker (את) have inadvertently dropped out and been replaced with the conjunction אֲשֶׁר, perhaps under the influence of the second line, or else the original sequence of consonants ירשׁ את has been corrupted to read

---

14. The annals of Sargon II identify the Israelite territory conquered as ᵘʳᵘ*Sa- mir-i-na gi-[mi]-ir É Ḫum-ri-a*, "Samaria and the entire land of Bīt-Ḫumria" (i.e., "house of Omri"). See *COS* 2.118G (p. 298).

15. See the discussion in Daniel I. Block, *Judges, Ruth* (NAC 6; Nashville: Broadman & Holman, 1999), 549 – 86.

16. Northern foes: Meshech, Tubal, Gomer, Beth Togarmah; southern foes: Paras, Cush, Put; eastern foes: Sheba, Dedan; western foes: Tarshish (Ezek 38:1 – 13). For discussion, Block, *Ezekiel Chapters 25 – 48*, 436 – 49.

17. West: Philistia (Zeph 2:4 – 7); east: Moab and Ammon (2:8 – 11); south: Ethiopia (2:12); north: Assyria (2:13 – 15).

18. This has led many to isolate this verse as a late gloss. See below.

19. Which involves dropping the first and last letters and reversing the order of the three that remain. A plausible alternative proposes that the parallelism suggests אֲשֶׁר be retained, and that the corruption involved the loss of a place name + verb, a counterpart to "in Sepharad, they will possess." See Raabe (*Obadiah*, 261 – 62). However, this overloads the first line, extending a sentence that is already unusually long. An argument for the restoration of the verb may also derive from the nature of Hebrew parallelism. Normally elliptical parallelism involves deletion of an element in the second line, rather than the first (cf. v. 19a-b; 19c-d).

Obadiah 20		
And as for the exiles of Halah	belonging to the people of Israel [they will dispossess]	the Canaanites as far as Zarephath;
And as for the exiles of Jerusalem	who are in Sepharad they will possess	the towns of the Negev.
כְּנַעֲנִים עַד־צָרְפַת	לִבְנֵי יִשְׂרָאֵל [וְיִרְשׁוּ אֵת]	וְגָלֻת הַחֵל־הַזֶּה
אֵת עָרֵי הַנֶּגֶב	אֲשֶׁר בִּסְפָרַד יִרְשׁוּ	וְגָלֻת יְרוּשָׁלַ͏ִם

אֲשֶׁר.[19] It also assumes that הַחֵל הַזֶּה, "this company," which makes little sense, represents a corruption of חֲלָה זֶה, "this Halah."

These are both marked sentences, departing from the normal verb + subject + object sequence. The construction involving waw conjunction + noun at the beginning of both sentences suggests the actions described here transpire in association with v. 19[20] and focuses the attention on the actors (the exiles) rather than the actions (the possession). The feminine noun גָּלוּת derives from a root גלה, "to leave, go into exile."[21] This noun is used both for the abstract notion of "exile, captivity"[22] or as a collective for "exiles."[23] The practice of expelling the populations of conquered cities and lands and relocating them elsewhere was widespread in the ANE. The policy was driven by several motives: (1) to punish the vanquished for resisting the invaders; (2) to destroy ethnic and national loyalties; (3) to remove those elements of the population who might lead in resistance movements against the occupiers; (4) to enslave the captives and provide human resources for projects elsewhere in the empire; (5) to bolster the economy elsewhere in the empire; and (6) to provide conscript personnel for the army.

In contrast to the people of the northern kingdom, who were scattered all over the Assyrian empire, the Judeans taken to Babylon by Nebuchadnezzar fared relatively well in exile. They were allowed to live in Jewish communities and were settled in areas so favorable that when Cyrus issued the decree in 539 BC that they could return to Jerusalem, only a small proportion did so (Ezra 2:1 – 70).

Obadiah's reference to the exiles continues his interest in greater Israel. In the first line of v. 20 he speaks of "the exiles … belonging to the people of Israel," an obvious allusion to the deportees from the northern kingdom carried off by the Assyrians in 722 – 721 BC; this reference adds credence to the emendation of the text to read "Halah." In 2 Kgs 17:6; 18:11; 1 Chr 5:26, this place is the location to which Israelites were deported and where they were settled. The location of Halah is unknown, but the association of the name with the River Habor (2 Kgs 17:6) suggests a place near Gozan on the Balikh River, one of the tributaries of the northern Euphrates.[24] The expression "people of Israel" (בְּנֵי יִשְׂרָאֵל; lit., "sons of Israel") occurs more than 600 times in the OT, which represents one fourth of all appearances of the name "Israel." Even more than expressions like "house of Jacob," "house of Joseph," and "house of Esau" (v. 18), this phrase reflects a sense of unity that transcends political considerations. It was founded on a conviction of consanguinity and kinship and on descent from a common ancestor.[25]

"The exiles of Jerusalem" in v. 20c represent the

20. JM §118f.
21. Isa 5:13; Jer 1:3; Lam 1:3; Ezek 39:23; Amos 1:5; 5:5; 6:7.
22. 2 Kgs 25:27 = Jer 52:31; Ezek.1:2; 33:21; 40:1.
23. Isa 20:4; 45:13; Jer 24:5; 28:4; 29:22; Amos 1:6, 9; Obad 20.

24. See further, Henry O. Thompson, "Halah," *ABD*, 3.25.
25. For full discussion, see Block, *Foundations of National Identity*, 153 – 201; also idem, "'Israel' — 'Sons of Israel': A Study in Hebrew Eponymic Usage," *Studies in Religion* 13 (1984): 301 – 26.

captives whom Nebuchadnezzar's army had carried off to Babylon in 586 BC.[26] However, the reference to exiles "who are in Sepharad" is puzzling. Four main candidates for its location have been proposed: Spain;[27] Hesperides in Cyrene, North Africa;[28] Separda in western Media;[29] and Sardis, the capital of the Lydian kingdom in Asia Minor. Scholars tend to find the last suggestion most persuasive, especially since the discovery of a fifth- to fourth-century BC bilingual Lydian-Aramaic inscription that identifies the city as ספרד, the very consonants we find here.[30]

However, the dating of the prophecies of Obadiah renders this view unlikely. According to the biblical records, the only specified destination for the deportees from Judah in 598–597 and 586 BC was Babylon.[31] Since the Babylonian empire did not include Lydia,[32] it is doubtful Nebuchadnezzar would have sent any deportees there. It is possible that a Jewish community was found in Sardis in

Obadiah's time, perhaps as merchandise in the slave trade involving Philistines and Phoenicians (Joel 4:4–6[3:4–6]) or the Edomites (Amos 1:6, 9).[33] However, it is unlikely Obadiah would have spoken of them as the גָּלוּת ("exiles" generally, or "the exiles of Jerusalem" in particular). Because the name "Sepharad" occurs only here, any attempt to identify the place is speculative. The context requires a location in Babylon. Either Sepharad is a cipher or code word for Babylon itself,[34] or it identifies the location of a specific place in Babylon where the exiles were settled.[35]

Obadiah's specification of territories to be reclaimed by the returned exiles from Halah and Babylon respectively fits the historical and geographic picture. The former, representing the northern kingdom of Israel, will dispossess[36] "the Canaanites as far as Zarephath." Zarephath identifies a coastal Phoenician city fourteen miles north of Tyre and eight miles south of Sidon (modern

---

26. The reference to the deportees as גָּלוּת יְרוּשָׁלַ͏ִם occurs also in Jer 40:1. Cf. also this same phrase as an expression for the "captivity of Jerusalem" in Jer 1:3.

27. Based on the Targumic reading אַסְפַּמְיָא, that is, Hispania. Since the Middle Ages the name Sepharad/ Sephardic has distinguished Jews from the Iberian Peninsula from Ashkenazi Jews of central Europe. For discussion, see David Neiman, "Sefarad: The Name of Spain," *JNES* 22 (1963): 128–32.

28. J. Gray, "The Diaspora of Israel and Judah in Obadiah v 20," *ZAW* 65 (1953): 53–59; Watts, *Obadiah*, 64. By this interpretation Sepharad represents a southern counterpart to the Israelite exiles in northern Halah.

29. Identified with *Šaparda* in the annals of Sargon II (*ARAB*, 2 §§11, 14, 147). Thus Stuart, *Hosea-Jonah*, 421.

30. See *KAI* 260:2. See further Renkema, *Obadiah*, 213–15; Raabe, *Obadiah*, 266–68.

31. 2 Kgs 24:10–16; 2 Chr 36:10, 20; Jer 29; 52:28–30; Ezek. 1:1–3; 3:15; the book of Daniel. Cf. 2 Kgs 25:11 and Jer 52:15 which do not specify the destination of the deportation.

32. Though his influence may have extended that far. See Donald J. Wiseman, *Nebuchadnezzar and Babylon* (Oxford: Oxford Univ. Press, 1985), 41, 83–84.

33. On slave trade between Tyre and Ionia (Greece) and

Asia Minor, see Ezek 27:13; on relations between Lydia and Tyre, see Ezek 27:10.

34. Like Shishak in Jer 26:26; 51:41, or Leb Kamai in Jer 51:1. The rabbis interpreted Shishak as an *athbash*, because it substitutes the last letter of the alphabet (*taw*) for the first (*aleph*) and the second last (*shin*) for the second (*beth*). See further, Jack R. Lundbom, *Jeremiah 21–36: A New Translation with Introduction and Commentary* (AB 21B; New York: Doubleday, 2004), 266.

35. Perhaps "the city of Judeans" (URU *šá* LÚ *ia-a-ḫu-du-a-a*) or "the city of Judah" ([URU]*ia-ḫu-du*, and variations) that has recently surfaced on a series of texts that refer to a location near the city of Babylon itself. The earliest text in this corpus dates to Nebuchadnezzar's 33rd year (572 BC) and another to Amel-Marduk's first year (561 BC), immediately prior to or during Obadiah's ministry. For discussion, see Laurie E. Pearce, "New Evidence for Judaeans in Babylonia," in *Judah and the Judaeans in the Persian Period* (ed. O. Lipschits and M. Oeming; Winona Lake, IN: Eisenbrauns, 2006), 399–411. Contra Renkema (*Obadiah*, 211–15), there is no need to treat v. 20 as a late insertion based on this name.

36. As noted earlier, when people are the object of the verb יָרַשׁ, it means "to dispossess" rather than "to possess."

Sarafand).[37] Since ancient Phoenicia consisted of a series of city states,[38] this location may explain why Obadiah named Zarephath as the representative city of the Phoenicians. According to the ideal boundaries of ancient Israel[39] and the tribal allotments, all of Phoenicia fell within the territory of Israel, with the coastal region being assigned to Asher (Josh 19:24 – 31). However, although the Danites seized the valley north of Lake Hula and southwest of Mount Hermon, the Israelites failed to conquer or occupy the coastal region (Judg 1:31). After the conquests of David and the incorporation of all tribes into his kingdom, the Phoenicians represented what remained of ancient Canaanite peoples.

Obadiah expresses awareness of this ethnic reality when he identifies the targets of the Israelites' advance as "Canaanites." This name is a gentilic, referring to the population that occupied the region called Canaan. According to biblical and extrabiblical evidence, in the Late Bronze Age the southern limits of the territory known as "Canaan" were defined by an arc drawn from the southeast corner of the Mediterranean Sea and the southern tip of the Dead Sea, while the northern limits lay to the south of the kingdoms of Ugarit and Alalakh.[40] With this statement Obadiah anticipates finally the realization of YHWH's ancient land promises to the patriarchs and to their descendants, the Israelites.

If the returned exiles from the northern kingdom extend control northward, it is appropriate that the returned exiles from Judah should move southward. Although in v. 19a "the Negev" functioned as a designation for the inhabitants of this region who would possess Mount Esau, here in v. 20d the name is used in its more common geographic sense. We should not imagine the "towns of the Negev" to be vast metropolitan centers;[41] this region could not support a great population. Rather, as is the case elsewhere, an עִיר refers fundamentally to a settlement with defensive walls and gate structures. To possess the cities of the Negev is equivalent to "possessing the gates of the enemy" (cf. Gen 22:17; 24:60). The Judahites' claim to the Negev signals the fulfillment of YHWH's ancient promise to grant his people the land as far south as the River of Egypt (Wadi el-Arish).

2. The Restoration of YHWH's Rule (v. 21)

If v. 17 is the climax of this short book, then v. 21 brings his proclamation to a triumphant conclusion. Having claimed all the territory originally allotted to Israel, their ascent of Mount Zion seals their position. Although the verb עָלָה, "to go up," often occurs in the context of worship, referring to processions of celebrants ascending the hill of Zion for a meeting with YHWH,[42] as frequently elsewhere here this verb bears military overtones. Since Israel's original conquest of Canaan involved the capture of fortified towns rather than pitched battles between two armies in the open field, this verb became idiomatic for "to attack," that is, to storm a stronghold on top of a hill.[43]

37. LXX *Sarepta* (also Luke 4:26); Neo-Assyrian texts, *Zariptu*. Zarepta is named elsewhere in the OT only in 1 Kgs 17:9 – 10.

38. The name "Phoenicia" never occurs in the Bible.

39. Gen 15:18 – 21; Exod 23:23 – 33; Num 34:1 – 29; Deut 11:24 – 25; Josh 1:3 – 4.

40. See further Richard S. Hess, "Occurrences of Canaan in Late Bronze Age Archives of the West Semitic World," in *Israel Oriental Studies 18: Past Links: Studies in the Languages and Cultures of the Ancient Near East* (ed. S. Izre'el, I. Singer, and R. Zadok; Winona Lake, IN: Eisenbrauns, 1998), 365 – 72.

41. Cf. LXX, τὰς πόλεις τοῦ Ναγεβ.

42. Exod 34:24; 1 Sam 10:3; Pss 24:3; 122:4; Isa 2:3; Jer 31:6; Mic 4:2.

43. Judg 1:1; 1 Kgs 20:22; Isa 7:1; etc.

This sense is confirmed here by the subject, "saviors."[44] Hebrew מוֹשִׁעִים is often used of persons who rescue the helpless from their desperate circumstance.[45] However, the present usage recalls Judg 3:9, 15, where the historian chooses this word to identify the major "judges" whom YHWH raised up to rescue (הוֹשִׁיעַ) the Israelites from the power of those whom he had sent to punish them for their rebellion against him.[46] Those who had been victims of enemy invaders but were brought back by YHWH will go on the offensive, and they will reclaim the most important stronghold in the land.

But the final phrase of v. 21a catches the reader/hearer by surprise: "to rule Mount Esau." Since the object of the infinitive לִשְׁפֹּט is a place rather than a person or a people group, as in the book of Judges the verb שָׁפַט means generally "to govern, rule," in contrast to the common judicial sense of "to judge."[47] From Mount Zion the "saviors" will govern Mount Esau. As in vv. 15b–16d, Esau seems to be representative for all the nations, which means that finally, in fulfillment of Deut 26:19 and 28:1, Israel will be high above all the nations of the earth; they will be the head and not the tail, and they will only be on top (לְמַעְלָה) and no longer underneath (לְמָטָּה; Deut 28:13). Although Mount Zion is usually portrayed as the locus from which YHWH rules the nations,[48] here the rulers are clearly the Israelite "saviors."

However, this does not mean that they achieve the ultimate prize on their own or that they seize the power over the nations. On the contrary, as the final clause of v. 21 declares, their ascent of Mount Zion and their governing of Esau give concrete expression to the kingship of YHWH, represented by the word הַמְּלוּכָה. This term may denote "the status of royalty" (Ezek 16:13), but it usually refers to the abstract notion of "kingship, rulership, dominion." Jezebel gives classic expression of the concept in her rebuke of Ahab: "Surely you exercise kingship over Israel" (1 Kgs. 21:7).[49] The present construction, וְהָיְתָה לַיהוה הַמְּלוּכָה expresses ownership; "the dominion will belong to YHWH."[50] But this is not one rulership among many; the definite article implies there is only one dominion that matters, and that dominion is YHWH's alone. Indeed the opening conjunction could be interpreted adversatively: saviors will go up to Mount Zion and govern Mount Esau, *but the rule* will be YHWH's. We find a close parallel to Obadiah's statement in Ps 22:28–29[27–28]:

> All the ends of the earth shall remember
>   and turn to YHWH;
> and all the families of the nations
>   shall [prostrate themselves] before him.
> For the dominion belongs to YHWH,
>   and he rules over the nations. (NRSV)

Obadiah hereby ends his prophecy by declaring the fulfillment of the longing of a generation that

---

44. Perhaps under the influence of v. 17a, LXX, Aquila, Theodotion, and the Syriac Peshitta translate the form as if it were a passive hophal participle, i.e., "those who have been redeemed." However, neither the hophal nor passive niphals of this verb ever occur in the OT.

45. Deut 22:27; 28:29, 31; Judg 12:3; 2 Sam 22:42; Isa 47:15.

46. Similarly 2 Kgs 13:5; Isa 19:20; 45:15.

47. As in Judg 3:10; 10:2–3; 12:7–14; 15:20; 16:31; 1 Sam 4:18; 8:5; 2 Kgs 15:5; 23:22; Isa 40:23; Amos 2:3; Pss 2:10; 94:2; 96:13; 148:11. This interpretation is reinforced by the usage of cognate expressions in Akkadian, Ugaritic, and Phoenician.

For fuller discussion, see Block, *Judges, Ruth*, 21–25.

48. Pss 47:8[7]; 102:12–15; 110:2; Isa 2:2–4; Mic 4:2–3; Zech 9:9–10.

49. Usually the expression refers to kingship over Israel: Saul (1 Sam 10:16; 11:14; 14:47; 18:8), David (1 Chr 10:14), Absalom (2 Sam 16:8), Adonijah (1 Kgs 2:15), Solomon (1:46; 2:15, 22), Jeroboam (11:35; 12:21), Ahab (21:7).

50. Compare Adonijah's comment to Solomon in 1 Kgs 2:15: "You know that the kingdom belonged to me [לִי הָיְתָה הַמְּלוּכָה], and all Israel expected me to be king."

thought it had witnessed YHWH's abdication of the throne and his defeat at the hands of Marduk. Those in exile may well have heard the Babylonians shouting at the Akitu (New Year's) Festival, "Marduk is king! Marduk is king!" They may even have observed the Babylonians celebrating Marduk's kingship with dramatizations and/or recitation of the *Enuma Elish*, which ends with the gods acknowledging his unrivaled lordship over them and his role as shepherd king over the people.[51]

Obadiah's declaration that the dominion belongs to YHWH is significant in several respects. First, it means that YHWH alone, not Marduk, the god of Babylon, or Chemosh, the god of the Moabites, or any other god determines the destiny of the nations. Second, it means that Israel is no longer subject to any earthly powers, but they answer only to YHWH, and they find their security in him. At the same time, it means that their history of rejection of his kingship (1 Sam 8:7) is finally over. Third, the unqualified nature of the statement suggests that YHWH is indeed king over all. He is not merely "king over Jeshurun" (Deut 33:5); he is king of the nations as well. If the Israelites exercise any control over Esau or the nations, it is not as kings over them, for theirs is a delegated rather than ultimate authority.

With this final declaration Obadiah joins in the refrain of psalmists[52] and prophets[53] declaring YHWH's cosmic and universal kingship, a theme that becomes especially prominent in the apocalyptic book of Daniel.[54] But the question remains: Does YHWH rule from the heavens, or does he rule from Zion? Obadiah does not offer a direct answer. In v. 17b he had declared that Mount Zion would be holy, implying [but only implying] the sanctifying presence of YHWH. Other prophets address the issue more directly. In Ezekiel's final vision, he saw the glory of YHWH returning to the temple and heard his kingship declared in unequivocally concrete terms: "Human, as for the place of my throne, and the place for the soles of my feet, where I will dwell in the midst of the sons of Israel forever" (Ezek 43:7).[55] When we link Obad 17 and 21, we may recognize in this prophecy a summary echo of a fuller statement in Joel:

> YHWH roars from Zion,
> and sounds his voice from Jerusalem,
> and the heavens and the earth shake.
> But YHWH is a refuge for his people,
> a stronghold for the people of Israel.
> So you will know that I am YHWH your God,
> Who dwells in Zion, my holy mountain.
> And Jerusalem will be holy,
> and strangers will never again pass through it.
> […]
> But Judah will be inhabited forever,
> and Jerusalem to all generations.
> I will avenge their blood,
> which I have not avenged,
> for YHWH dwells in Zion.
> (Joel 4:16–17, 20–21[3:16–17, 20–21])

Remarkably, like Obadiah, Joel sees these events transpiring after YHWH has punished Edom for their violence to the Judahites and for other murderous crimes. However, unlike Joel, who spends a great deal of time on the rejuvenating effects of YHWH's restorative acts on the landscape (Joel 2:18–27; 4:18[3:18]), Obadiah expresses no interest at all in the ecological effects of the kingship of YHWH.

51. *COS* 1.111 (pp. 401–2).

52. Pss 24:8–10; 29:10; 47:3[2]; 93:1–5; 95:3–5; 96:1–10; 97:1–6; 98:6; 103:19–20.

53. Jer 10:6–10; 46:18; 48:15; 51:57; Zech 14:9, 16–17; Mal 1:14.

54. Dan 2:47; 3:33[4:3]; 4:14, 22, 31–34[17, 25, 34–37]; 5:18–24; 6:27–28[26–27]; 7:9–14, 26–27.

55. As translated by Block, *Ezekiel Chapters 25–48*, 575.

Canonical and Practical Significance

Having worked our way through the book of Obadiah, we may now reflect on the book's canonical and theological significance. The brevity of the book masks its profundity.

The Role of Edom in the Israel's History

Elsewhere only the book of Nahum, which is identified as "an oracle [מַשָּׂא] concerning Nineveh" (Nah 1:1 NRSV), is consumed entirely with a foreign nation. Considering the significance of the Assyrians in the divine program relating to Israel,[1] this is not surprising. But why should an entire book be concerned with Edom, a minor player in the ANE historical drama? Other prophets direct oracles of equal length or greater length to foreign nations, but they are for the most part directed against the major players: Egypt, Babylon, and Tyre.[2] The only exception is the major oracle against the third rate nation of Moab in Jer 48. But these are all embedded in larger collections consisting of many and varied prophecies.

Since we have none of Obadiah's other prophecies, it is remarkable that this singular oracle should have been preserved, presumably originally on its own scroll. The conservation of the book itself speaks to its theological significance. Edom may have been a small player on the ancient international stage, but the book reinforces the impression created in the biblical narratives, the Psalter, and the Prophets that the descendants of Esau actually played a major role in Israel's history.[3] In fulfillment of the patriarch Isaac's verbal testament in Gen 27:39 – 40, the Edomites had served Israel (2 Sam 8:11 – 14; 1 Kgs 11:14 – 16; 2 Kgs 3:8 – 27), but they had also broken free (1 Kgs 11:17 – 22; 2 Kgs 8:20 – 22). Balaam, the prophet from Mesopotamia, had anticipated Edom's ultimate demise, apparently at the hand of Israel (Num 24:18 – 19),

---

1. Which may underlie the narrator of Jonah characterizing Nineveh as "a great city to God" (עִיר־גְּדוֹלָה לֵאלֹהִים, 3:3). Remarkably no book is directed entirely against Babylon.

2. Compared with Obadiah's 291 words, note Isa 13 – 14 (Babylon, 520 words); Isa 19 (Egypt, 327 words); Jer 46 (Egypt, 403 words); Jer 48 (Moab, 591 words); Ezek 26 – 28 (Tyre, 961 words); Ezek 29 – 32 (Egypt, 1485 words).

3. References to Esau or Edom/Edomites occur in Genesis, Exodus, Numbers, Deuteronomy, Joshua, Judges, 1 and 2 Samuel, 1 and 2 Kings, 1 and 2 Chronicles, the Psalms, Lamentations, Isaiah, Jeremiah, Ezekiel, Daniel, Joel, Amos, Obadiah, and Malachi.

though shortly thereafter Moses had reminded his people that YHWH had granted Mount Seir to the descendants of Esau just as he would give to Israel the land of Canaan (Deut 2:4 – 7, 22).

Edom's significance to the biblical narratives is reflected in Gen 36:1 – 43, where we find a genealogical register of the descendants of Esau that is without parallel for non-Israelites in the OT.[4] The Edomites' involvement in international politics in the seventh to sixth centuries is attested not only in Ps 137:7 and in the prophetic oracles against them,[5] but particularly in Jer 27:1 – 3, which reports Edom's involvement in an international alliance against the Babylonian overlords.

Based on data from several extrabiblical sources, we may now place Obadiah's oracle within the history of the nation of Edom. Although Egyptian references to Seir date to the fourteenth to twelfth centuries BC,[6] the earliest references to Edom ('-d-w-m) occur in a late thirteenth-century BC letter from a frontier official to his superior.[7] The nation's significance is reflected also in neo-Assyrian records, which report that beginning in the early eighth century BC, along with other nations in the region, Edom (U-du-mu) dutifully paid tribute to Assyrian kings.[8] However, during the reign of Sargon II (721 – 705 BC), they joined Moab, Philistia, and Judah in an unsuccessful revolt against the Assyrians.[9] Edom later paid tribute to Sennacherib (704 – 681 BC),[10] and the Edomite king Qosgabri is recognized as a loyal vassal of Esarhaddon (680 – 669 BC) and Ashiurbanipal (668 – 627 BC), even providing the latter with troops for his campaign against Egypt.[11] As noted earlier, the ultimate demise of Edom is reflected in the annals of the Babylonian king Nabonidus (555 – 539 BC), who laid siege to the "town of Edom" — apparently a reference to Bozrah, its capital.[12]

Edom as a Representative of the Nations

However, to Obadiah the sons of Esau represented much more than a minor ANE nation or even the relatives of the Israelites; he links the demise of Edom with the "day of YHWH" that is approaching for all nations, so that the Edomites function as a representative of all the nations arrayed against YHWH and his people. In so doing Obadiah picks up on Amos, who predicted that YHWH would raise up the fallen

---

4. Some of the information found in Gen 36 is repeated in 1 Chr 1:35 – 54. In contrast to the detail of the lists of Edomite/ Seirite descendants and kings, 1 Chr 1:29 – 33 traces the descendants of his sons Ishmael and Jokshan and Midian only one generation further.

5. Isa 34:5 – 17; Jer 49:7 – 22; Ezek 25:12 – 14; 35:1 – 15; Amos 1:11 – 12.

6. Early 14th century, Tell el-Amarna tablets (*ANET*, 488); 13th century, Ramesses II inscriptions (Bartlett, *Edom*, 77);

12th century, Ramesses III inscriptions (*ANET*, 262).

7. *ANET*, 259.

8. Adad-Nirari (810 – 783 BC; *ANET*, 281); Tiglath-Pileser III (744 – 727 BC; *ANET*, 282).

9. *ANET*, 287.

10. Ibid.

11. Ibid., 294.

12. Thus Bartlett, *Edom*, 157 – 651; cf. *ANET*, 305.

Isaiah's First Oracle against Edom

¹Draw near, O nations, to hear;
　　O peoples, give heed!
Let the earth hear, and all that fills it;
　　the world, and all that comes from it.
²For the Lord is enraged against all the nations,
　　and furious against all their hoards;
　　he has doomed them, has given them over for slaughter.
³Their slain shall be cast out,
　　and the stench of their corpses shall rise;
　　the mountains shall flow with their blood.
⁴All the host of heaven shall rot away,
　　and the skies roll up like a scroll.
All their host shall wither like a leaf withering on a vine,
　　or fruit withering on a fig tree.
⁵When my sword has drunk its fill in the heavens,
　　lo, it will descend upon Edom,
　　upon the people I have doomed to judgment [חֶרְמִי לְמִשְׁפָּט].
⁶The Lord has a sword; it is sated with blood,
　　it is gorged with fat,
　　with the blood of lambs and goats,
　　with the fat of the kidneys of rams.
For the Lord has a sacrifice in Bozrah,
　　a great slaughter in the land of Edom.
⁷Wild oxen shall fall with them,
　　and young steers with the mighty bulls.
Their land shall be soaked with blood,
　　and their soil made rich with fat.
⁸For the Lord has *a day of vengeance*,
　　a year of vindication by Zion's cause.
⁹And the streams of Edom shall be turned into pitch,
　　and her soil into sulfur;
　　her land shall become burning pitch.
¹⁰Night and day it shall not be quenched;
　　its smoke shall go up forever.
From generation to generation it shall lie waste;
　　no one shall pass through it forever and ever.
　　　　　　　　　　(Isa 34:1–10 NRSV, emphasis added)

booth of David that they might possess "the remnant of Edom" and all the nations who are called by YHWH's name (Amos 9:11 – 12).

However, Isaiah had developed this notion much more fully in a lengthy oracle (Isa 34 – 35) ostensibly directed toward the nations. However, the oracle has its crosshairs set on Edom, predicting specifically the destruction of Edom on YHWH's "day of vengeance" (34:8 – 9) in the context of the restoration and renewal of Zion. The prophet describes in detail how the land of Edom, including the surrounding desert and the Arabah, will become a paradise for the wild animals and a holy and secure dwelling place for the redeemed (34:11 – 35:9). Meanwhile Zion itself will become a place of everlasting joy.

But this is not the last word about Edom in the book of Isaiah. A later oracle (Isa 63:1 – 6) portrays Edom not only as the object of YHWH's fury, but also as the geographic origin of the one who comes to redeem his people. Playing on the root אדם, "red," the prophet declared their end. As in Isaiah, to Obadiah Edom represents all who stand in opposition to YHWH and who abuse his people, and the picture he paints of Edom's demise is paradigmatic of YHWH's ultimate vindication of his people and his triumph over all who oppose him.

Edom as Representative of Humanity

Moreover, Edom is also representative of all humanity. Just as the sons of Jacob and the sons of Esau are descended from Abraham and Isaac, so the Scriptures perceive all humanity as a consanguineous family, descendants of a common ancestor Adam, whose name (אָדָם) is cognate to Edom (אֱדוֹם). However, instead of being our "brother's keeper" (Gen 4:9), like Cain, the members of this family often stifle their natural affections and commit violent acts against each other. Even if we are not guilty of the crimes ourselves, we tend to clap our hands with gleeful *Schadenfreude* when others do so. Whether or not Herod the Great was an actual descendant of the original Edomites, the reputation for individual violence against one's family members finds its nadir in this son of Antipator I the Idumean. Not sparing "even the survivors whom he regarded as dearest to him" (Jos. *Ant.* 16.404), Herod had several members of his own family executed, including his wife Mariamme (*Ant.* 15.222 – 39) and his two sons by her, Alexander and Aristobulus (*Ant.* 16.392 – 94).[13]

This ethic of violence even toward one's own family is the antithesis of the ethic called for in YHWH's covenant with his people. They are not only to love their neighbors — their fellow citizens — as themselves (Lev 19:18), but they are also to demonstrate the same love to the sojourners (אֱדוֹם) as they do to their blood rela-

---

13. For Josephus's reflections on these horrendous crimes against "his own flesh and blood," see *Ant.* 16.395 – 404.

Isaiah's Second Oracle against Edom

[1]"Who is this that comes from Edom [אֱדוֹם]
    from Bozrah in garments stained crimson?
Who is this so splendidly robed,
    marching in his great might?"
"It is I, announcing vindication,
    mighty to save."
[2]"Why are your robes red [אָדֹם],
    and your garments like theirs who tread the wine press?"
[3]"I have trodden the wine press alone,
    and from the peoples no one was with me;
I trod them in my anger
    and trampled them in my wrath;
their juice spattered on my garments,
    and stained all my robes.
[4]For the day of vengeance was in my heart,
    and the year for my redeeming work had come.
[5]I looked, but there was no helper;
    I stared, but there was no one to sustain me;
so my own arm brought me victory,
    and my wrath sustained me.
[6]I trampled down peoples in my anger,
    I crushed them in my wrath,
    and I poured out their lifeblood on the earth." (Isa 63:1 – 6 NRSV)

tives (אֶזְרָח; Lev 19:34; cf. v. 18; Deut 10:19). When abused, God's people are to return evil with good, and in so doing will heap coals of fire on the heads of their enemies (Prov 25:20 – 22). This is the ethic of Jesus (Matt 5:43 – 48) and Paul (Rom 12:20). Of course, Jesus himself is the paradigmatic incarnation of this covenant love, even at the cost of his own life (Phil 2:5 – 8).

The Dominion Belongs to YHWH

The theological significance of the book of Obadiah extends far beyond its witness to Edom's place in history and their role as representatives of fundamental human depravity. This book offers a full-orbed vision of YHWH, climaxing in the final statement, "The dominion will belong to YHWH." But what does this book tell us about the reign of YHWH and about the character of this king?

First, Obadiah declares that YHWH announces his reign through authorized messengers. The book opens with a report of an envoy from the court of YHWH calling on the nations to rise up in battle against Edom, to which they willingly respond (v. 1). But Obadiah himself is one of these envoys who has access to the counsel of YHWH. In Deut 18:15–22 Moses had identified three features that would mark the badge of true prophets.

(1) They would be prophets after the order of Moses, into whose mouth YHWH would put his words and who would then speak for him (18:18).

(2) They would speak in the name of YHWH, which meant that to reject their word was to reject YHWH. Of course, these first two features could easily be forged. Jeremiah and Ezekiel spoke of self-inspired false prophets who claimed to run and speak for YHWH, but the visions they declared arose from their own imaginations (Jer 23:16–40; Ezek 13:1–7). By contrast, true prophets stand in the council of YHWH (עָמַד בְּסוֹד יהוה) to hear the words they are to proclaim and to be commissioned to proclaim them (Jer 23:18, 22). Just as an earthly monarch would authorize trusted counselors to stamp official documents with his seal, so YHWH puts into true prophets' mouths the verbal seals. Only he could authorize anyone to use the prophetic formulas that we find in Obadiah (vv. 1b, 4d, 8b, 18g).[14] The four occurrences of these formulas confirm Obadiah's status as a man carried along by the Holy Spirit and authorized to speak for God (2 Pet. 1:21).

(3) According to Deut 18:15–22, the third mark of true prophets was fulfilled predictions. YHWH's ability to predict events in the distant future and then to fulfill those prognostications distinguished him from all other gods (Isa 46:8–11). It did not take long for Obadiah's prophecies concerning Edom to transpire. The chronicles of Nabonidus suggest that the announced judgment on Edom was fulfilled in 553 BC, when the Babylonian king conquered Edom. Although the Idumeans of Jesus' day may have had some Edomite blood coursing through their veins, after the sixth century Edom as a nation ceased to exist. And unlike the sons of Jacob, the nation has never been resurrected.

The beginning of the fulfillment of Obadiah's promised restoration of Israel and Zion followed soon thereafter. It was satisfied in small measure when Cyrus issued a decree in 538 BC that the exiles in Babylon could return to Jerusalem and rebuild the temple (2 Chr 36:22–23; Ezra 1:1–4).[15] However, this never became the wholesale

---

14. These include the citation formula with YHWH as the subject, "Thus says Adonay YHWH" (כֹּה אָמַר אֲדֹנָי יהוה [v. 1b]); the divine declaration formula, "for YHWH has spoken" (כִּי יהוה דִּבֵּר [v. 18g]); and the signatory formula, "the declaration of YHWH" (נְאֻם יהוה [vv. 4d, 8b]). On these and other prophetic formulas, see Block, *Ezekiel Chapters 1–24*, 32–36.

15. The Cyrus Cylinder inscription in the British Museum demonstrates that Cyrus's congenial policy toward the Jews was part of a general policy toward nations that his predecessors the Babylonians had conquered. For translations of the document, see *ANET*, 315–16; *COS* 2.124 (p. 314).

restoration envisioned by other prophets like Ezekiel in Ezek 34 – 48. (1) Although 50,000 returned from exile (Ezra 2), this was a small fraction of the descendants of the twelve tribes scattered throughout the ancient world. (2) Although the Jews returned to the Promised Land, they occupied only a small region around Jerusalem. (3) Although they rebuilt the temple, it was an unimpressive project, and in any case the glory of YHWH never returned (Hag 1 – 2). (4) Although Zerubbabel, a Davidide, had been granted some authority in Jerusalem, he was only a governor, still under the suzerainty of Persia. But the restoration of 538 BC represented a down payment of the ultimate restoration and a reminder that YHWH had not forgotten his ancient covenant commitments to Abraham and his descendants.

Obadiah's vision of Jacob's restoration reiterates what he must have known from Isaiah, Jeremiah, and Ezekiel. However, its roots are found in Pentateuchal promises, most notably in YHWH's own promise of restoration after judgment in Lev 26:40 – 45, in Moses' reiteration and development of this theme in Deut 4:30 – 31; 30:1 – 10, and in the clear declaration in Israel's national anthem, Deut 32:34 – 43. In the end YHWH's memory of his irrevocable commitment to Israel and his compassion for his people would triumph (4:30 – 31).

Obadiah demonstrates YHWH's kingship by bringing down the high and exalting the low. Some modern readers who do not take into account the background to the book are offended by Obadiah's strong ethnic focus and his announcement of the elimination of an entire population. Is this not divinely sanctioned and divinely inflicted genocide? To the question we may offer three responses. (1) The Edomites are presented here as individuals, members of a family, who have collectively violated their brother when they should have protected him. (2) The violence toward Jacob was only one manifestation of an overweening pride. Like Adam's arrogant act of rebellion in Gen 3, so the sons of Esau's actions called for their punishment. (3) This treatment of Edom is consistent with YHWH's response to others who stood in opposition to him. In Deut 7 – 8 Moses had declared that if the Israelites would forget their God and behave like Canaanites, they too would experience this fate — which they eventually had at the hands of the Babylonians in 586 BC. The demise of Edom is not merely the consequence of a capricious and violent God's anger; it is his response to evil, a notion few modern readers understand.

YHWH's response to Edom concretizes the image that Hannah had expressed so eloquently centuries earlier in her oracular prayer (1 Sam 2:1 – 10) and that Mary would echo centuries later in her Magnificat (Luke 1:46 – 55). The bold font highlights the parallel treatment of the motif of raising the low and bringing down the high:

Hannah's Prayer (1 Sam 2:1 – 10)	Mary's Magnificat (Luke 1:46 – 55)

[1]My heart exults in the Lord;
    my strength is exalted in my God.
    My mouth derides my enemies,
    because I rejoice in my victory.
[2]There is no Holy One like the Lord,
    no one besides you;
    there is no Rock like our God.
[3]Talk no more so very proudly,
    let not arrogance come from your mouth;
    for the Lord is a God of knowledge,
    and by him actions are weighed.
[4]The bows of the mighty are broken,
    but the feeble gird on strength.
[5]Those who were full have hired themselves out for bread,
    but those who were hungry are fat with spoil.
    The barren has borne seven,
    but she who has many children is forlorn.
[6]The Lord kills and brings to life;
    he brings down to Sheol and raises up.
[7]The Lord makes poor and makes rich;
    he brings low, he also exalts.
[8]He raises up the poor from the dust;
    he lifts the needy from the ash heap,
    to make them sit with princes
    and inherit a seat of honor.
    For the pillars of the earth are the Lord's,
    and on them he has set the world.
[9]He will guard the feet of his faithful ones,
    but the wicked shall be cut off in darkness;
    for not by might does one prevail.
[10]The Lord! His adversaries shall be shattered;
    the Most High will thunder in heaven.
    The Lord will judge the ends of the earth;
    he will give strength to his king,
    and exalt the power of his anointed. (NRSV)
	[46]My soul magnifies the Lord,
	[47]and my spirit rejoices in God my Savior,
	[48]for he has looked with favor on the lowliness of his servant.
	    Surely, from now on all generations will call me blessed;
	[49]for the Mighty One has done great things for me,
	    and holy is his name.
	[50]His mercy is for those who fear him
	    from generation to generation.
	[51]He has shown strength with his arm;
	    he has scattered the proud in the thoughts of their hearts.
	[52]He has brought down the powerful from their thrones,
	    and lifted up the lowly;
	[53]he has filled the hungry with good things,
	    and sent the rich away empty.
	[54]He has helped his servant Israel,
	    in remembrance of his mercy,
	[55]according to the promise he made to our ancestors,
	    to Abraham and to his descendants forever. (NRSV)

Closer to Obadiah's time, Ezekiel had summarized the same principle in Ezek 17:24:

> I bring down the tall tree;
>   I exalt the low tree.
> I cause the green tree to wither,
>   and make the withered tree thrive.
> I am YHWH. I have spoken;
>   and I will perform.

Ezekiel also offered a concrete illustration of the principle in his oracles against Tyre in 28:1 – 19.

Isaiah 14:12 – 15

[12]How you are fallen from heaven,
  O Day Star, son of Dawn!
How you are cut down to the ground,
  you who laid the nations low!
[13]You said in your heart,
  "I will ascend to heaven;
I will raise my throne
  above the stars of God;
I will sit on the mount of assembly
  on the heights of Zaphon;
[14]I will ascend to the tops of the clouds,
  I will make myself like the Most High."
[15]But you are brought down to Sheol,
  to the depths of the Pit. (NRSV)

Although Obadiah shows some influence from Ezekiel, his characterization of Edom's overweening pride as smugness of heart and setting his nest among the stars links this passage particularly with Isaiah's portrayal of the star of the morning in Isa 14:12 – 15. Adapting this theme, and borrowing heavily from Jeremiah, as we have noted in the commentary, Obadiah speaks of YHWH's making Esau small among the nations (Obad 2), responding to his arrogance and smugness by bringing this one who claims to live among the stars back down to earth (vv. 3 – 4).[16]

---

16. Note the use of הוֹרִיד, "to bring down," which links this text verbatim with Jer 49:16, but the hophal form also occurs in Isa 14:15. Hannah and Ezekiel use a different expression, הִשְׁפִּיל, "to make low."

Christ the King in Obadiah

Although Obadiah's vision of Israel's future involves three of the promissory pillars on which the Israelites had based their security prior to their demise[17] (regathering the exiles, their reoccupation of the Promised Land, and YHWH's restoration of the sanctity of Jerusalem/Zion as his holy city), remarkably he says nothing about David or the restoration of his throne. He develops Hannah's motif of bringing down the high and mighty, but the prophet drops the climactic final verse of her prayer. Whether or not this book preserves only a fragment of the prophet's utterances, the absence of any reference to a Davidic Messiah represents a departure from Obadiah's prophetic predecessors and indeed from extrabiblical analogues.[18] In their vision of Israel's renewal, YHWH's eternal covenant with David was a key feature.[19]

Ezekiel 34 portrays YHWH as the divine shepherd gathering his sheep, who have been scattered by their own abusive shepherds, leading them to his abundant pasture, and then administering justice among them. Having reestablished the covenantal triangle involving himself, his people, and the land, YHWH introduces a second shepherd, his servant David, who will be prince among his people and feed them. The oracle concludes with an effusive description of the benefits of the covenant of peace that YHWH makes with them (34:20 – 24; cf. 37:21 – 28). This Davidic shepherd plays no role in the restoration itself, but once this has occurred, he occupies a central place in the picture. By contrast Obadiah's focus is entirely on YHWH as the one to whom the dominion (הַמְּלוּכָה) belongs. In the OT YHWH exercises kingship over Israel,[20] but he is also king of the cosmos.[21] In portraying YHWH as governing the affairs of the nations in the interests of his own people, Obadiah combines these two dimensions.

The motif of the kingship of God is not only common in the OT, but it also carries over into the NT. Not surprisingly, within the Trinity the Father is presented as king,[22] but it is fascinating to observe what happens to this motif in relation to Jesus.

---

17. See Figure 1.2, p. 34.

18. On this motif and this sequence of events in ANE texts, see Daniel I. Block, "Divine Abandonment: Ezekiel's Adaptation of an Ancient Near Eastern Motif," in *Perspectives on Ezekiel: Theology and Anthropology* (ed. Margaret S. Odell and John T. Strong; SBLSymS 9; Atlanta: Scholars, 2000), 15 – 42; idem, *The Gods of the Nations: Studies in Ancient Near Eastern National Theology* (rev. ed.; ETS Monograph; Grand Rapids: Baker, 2000), 113 – 46.

19. See Isa 9:6 – 7; 11:1 – 10; Jer 23:5 – 8; 33:14 – 16; Ezek 34:23 – 24; 37:15 – 23; Hos 3:5; Amos 9:11 – 12; Mic 5:1 – 5.

20. Deut 33:5; 1 Sam 8:7; 12:12; Isa 41:21; 44:6; 52:7; Ezek 20:33; Zeph 3:15; cf. Pss 10:16; 29:10; 44:5[4]; 146:10; 149:2.

21. Note esp. the divine kingship psalms, Pss 22:29[28]; 24:7 – 10; 47:3 – 9[2 – 8]; 48:32; 93:1 – 5; 95:3 – 5; 96:1 – 10;

97:1 – 6; 98:6; 103:19 – 22; and in the prophets, Jer 10:6 – 10; 46:18; 48:15; 51:57; Zech 14:9, 16 – 17; Mal 1:14. The theme of YHWH's kingship/dominion is especially prominent in Daniel: Dan 2:20 – 23, 47; 3:33[4:3]; 4:14, 22, 31 – 34 [17, 25, 34 – 37]; 5:18 – 24; 6:27 – 28[26 – 27]; 7:9 – 14, 26 – 27. In Daniel Yahweh is declared to be the king over all, but he exercises his sovereignty particularly in the interests of his people. Even though orthodox Israelites perceived Yahweh as the universal monarch, the treatment of Zion as the seat of his rule is analogous to the Babylonian treatment of Marduk as king in their city. Ps 68:25[24]; Isa 24:23. Notice the emphasis on the eternal nature of Yahweh's kingdom in Pss 29:10; 145:1 – 3; 146:10; Jer 10:10; Dan 2:44; 3:33[4:3], 31[34]; 6:27[26]; 7:27.

22. See the Lord's Prayer, Matt 6:9 – 13; also Rev 4:1 – 11;

As summarized in Acts 2:36, concerning Jesus the NT makes two principal points.[23] (1) He was the messianic Son of David, who had come to establish YHWH's rule over Israel and to extend that rule to the entire world. But Obadiah does not speak of a royal Messiah. (2) Jesus is YHWH incarnate, which identifies him with the covenant God of Israel, who was also the creator of all things.

The gospel of Matthew begins by naming Jesus Immanuel ("God with us," Matt 1:23) and ends with his climactic declaration, "All authority in heaven and on earth has been given to me" (28:18). The gospel of John begins with John the Baptizer heralding the arrival of the great king (John 1:23), "I am the voice of one calling in the wilderness, 'Make straight the way for the Lord [Gk *kyrios*; a quotation of Isa 40:3, where the Heb reads יהוה]." This gospel ends with Jesus commissioning Peter to "take care of [shepherd] my sheep" (John 21:16), an obvious allusion to Ezek 34:30 – 31, where YHWH is the Shepherd-King.[24]

Paul's beautiful *Carmen Christi* ("Hymn to Christ") ends with a glorious statement about Jesus Christ (Phil 2:9 – 11):

> Therefore God exalted him to the highest place
> > and gave him the name that is above every name,
> that at the name of Jesus every knee should bow,
> > in heaven and on earth and under the earth,
> and every tongue acknowledge that Jesus Christ is Lord [Gk κύριος; Heb יהוה]
> > to the glory of God the Father. (NIV)

In Col 1:15 – 17 Paul declares that Jesus' cosmic supremacy antedates the creation of the world:

> He is the image of the invisible God,
> > the firstborn of all creation;
> for in him all things in heaven and on earth were created,
> > things visible and invisible,
> > whether thrones or dominions or rulers or powers —
> all things have been created through him and for him.
> He himself is before all things,
> > and in him all things hold together.[25]

---

etc., and the frequent references to "the kingdom of God" (Matt 6:33; 12:28; etc.).

23. "Therefore let all Israel be assured of this: God has made this Jesus, whom you crucified, both Lord [Gk *kyrios*; read Heb *yhwh*] and Christ [Messiah]."

24. On "shepherd" as a royal metaphor, see J. A. Soggin, "ראה to tend," *TLOT*, 3:1247 – 48.

25. This is the NRSV translation, formatted in a poetic manner. Note also Eph 1:19b – 23: "That power is the same as the mighty strength he exerted when he raised Christ from the dead and seated him at his right hand in the heavenly realms, far above all rule and authority, power and dominion, and every name that is invoked, not only in the present age but also in the one to come. And God placed all things under his feet and appointed him to be head over everything for the church, which is his body, the fullness of him who fills everything in every way" (NIV).

Elsewhere Jesus' cosmic dominion is reflected in his superlative titles. In 1 Tim 6:14–15, Paul refers to Jesus as "our Lord [κύριος] Jesus Christ … the blessed and only Ruler [μόνος δυνάστης], the King of kings [ὁ βασιλεὺς τῶν βασιλευόντων] and Lord of lords [κύριος τῶν κυριευόντων]" (NIV).[26] "Lord of lords" translates Hebrew אֲדֹנֵי הָאֲדֹנִים, which in the OT is applied only to YHWH.[27] The portrayal of Jesus as king over all climaxes in Revelation in the doxologies of the angels who surround the throne and all living creatures in heaven and on earth:

> Worthy is the Lamb, who was slain,
>> to receive power and wealth and wisdom and strength
>> and honor and glory and praise.…
> To him who sits on the throne and to the Lamb
>> be praise and honor and glory and power,
>>> for ever and ever! (Rev 5:12–13 NIV).[28]

And herein lies the key to the significance of the book of Obadiah for Christian readers. In Christ not only the prophecy of Obadiah, but all of God's promises to Israel are fulfilled. In Christ Gentile believers are grafted into the vine and made heirs of those promises (Rom 11:17–24). In Christ the high and mighty are cast down and the humble are exalted. In Christ God vanquishes the kingdom of darkness and all who stand in opposition to him and his people (Col 2:15). In Christ citizens of the kingdom of darkness and sin are delivered and ushered into the kingdom of light (Col 1:13). In Christ those who like Israel deserve judgment for their rebellion and sin are reconciled to God (2 Cor 5:19). The dominion belongs to YHWH incarnate in Jesus Christ! To him be the glory and dominion for ever and ever. Amen!

---

26. The latter two titles, "King of kings and Lord of lords," occur also in Rev 17:14 and 19:16.

27. Note esp. Deut 10:17, "For YHWH your God is God of gods and Lord of lords, the great God, mighty and awesome." Cf. also Ps 136:3.

28. Cf. also the doxology at the end of Jude: "To him who is able to keep you from stumbling and to present you before his glorious presence without fault and with great joy— to the only God our Savior be glory, majesty, power and authority, through Jesus Christ our Lord, before all ages, now and forevermore! Amen." (Jude 1:24–25 NIV).

Scripture Index

Note that for all entries in which there is variation in versification between the Hebrew Bible and the English Bible, the Hebrew versification is first and the English versification is in brackets.

Subject Index

Author Index